THE BANQUET

EXPLORING THE GREATEST
INVITATION EXTENDED TO HUMANITY

- RONALD J. MAHLER -

THE BANQUET

Printed in Canada
ISBN 978-1-988928-03-6 Soft Cover
ISBN 978-1-988928-04-3 E-book

Published by: Castle Quay Books
Burlington, Ontario
Tel: (416) 573-3249
E-mail: info@castlequaybooks.com | www.castlequaybooks.com

Edited by Marina Hofman Willard and Lori Mackay
Cover design and book interior by Burst Impressions
Printed at Essence Publishing, Belleville, Ontario

Library and Archives Canada Cataloguing in Publication

Mahler, Ron, 1967-, author
The Banquet : exploring the greatest invitation extended to humanity / Ronald James Mahler.

ISBN 978-1-988928-03-6 (softcover)

1. Lord's Supper. I. Title.

BV825.3.M34 2018 234'.163 C2018-901602-7

To my sister Linda, who has always had food on the table,
room around it, and a house filled with love
for anyone who enters.

A CHAIR

—RONALD J. MAHLER

Tables' mantling unequalled fair
Their settings sprawling, remarkable
Upright and wanting, is a single, vacant chair
Its placement among rows of the thankful

In a room majestic and perceptively endless
Voices meld together in wonderful flight
Love, like a prism, magnified and tremendous
Embodied in the One who sits in perfect light

Curtains rise, exposing a Banquet Divine
Dishes plentiful and elevating appetites
Senses delight in working overtime
Yet a single chair remains, void of its invite.

"Here I am! I stand at the door and knock.
If anyone hears my voice and opens the door,
I will come in and eat with that person,
and they with me."
—*Jesus Christ*

(REVELATION 3:20)

CONTENTS

INTRODUCTION

People are naturally curious about the afterlife. During our childhood years, many of us are taught that there is a blissful place that "good" people go to after they die: heaven. However, many of our cultural conceptions about the reality of heaven and how one gets there are either askew of the Bible's teaching or estranged from it.

Many parables of Jesus Christ underscore the reality of hell while highlighting how one can avoid going there or how one can enter the kingdom of God and experience its heavenly rewards for eternity. Jesus's parable of the great banquet—a foreshadowing of what the Bible refers to as the marriage feast of the Lamb—addresses this all-important subject with sobriety.

In the parable (Luke 14:15–24), the Lord relays how a servant is sent by his wealthy and benevolent master to tell those he has already invited to a celebratory feast that the banquet is now ready. Incredibly, everyone who has been invited doesn't actually want to attend. Their decision infuriates the goodly master, and so he directs his servant to invite others outside of the privileged crowd the master had at the top of his invitation list. The servant obeys, and the doors of the banquet are held open for people whom the initial invitees wouldn't think to invite to their own feasts and banquets. So heartbroken and angered is the master as a result of the initial invitees' ungrateful attitude towards his kindness that he declares that none of this crowd will be permitted to snatch even a morsel from the bounty of his banquet's table.

As we'll see, the parable of the great banquet's characters indeed have "real-life" identities attached to them, just as the parable's punchline points to the eternal rewards in heaven that await those who believe in the Son of God, as contrasted with the equally eternal (yet tragic) consequences that accompany others' *unbelief* and ultimate rejection of God's Son. The parable invites the reader to contemplate its narrative as motivation for one to do everything necessary in order to get on this banquet's list of invitees!

By all biblical accounts, this event will be unlike anything we could possibly experience in the here and now. Imagine walking into an elaborately decorated regal hall resembling the length of countless football fields buttressed together. Imagine how overwhelmed you feel as your eye scans an enormous exhibition of faces, voices, ethnic groups, colours, and excitement. You are speechless because no words can fill in the blanks of what you could never have known about heaven. It's impossible to process all you *can* see or to appreciate the layers of lavish fare that extend throughout and adorn the space's hemispheric sightlines.

Such are the optical titillations inherent within the biblical imagery of God uniting around His heavenly banquet table with all the redeemed of every age and of every racial background, language, social status, and nation the world has known. In "the New Jerusalem," the house of God and the family of faith are joined together in what Matthew Henry referred to as "a reception for repentant sinners."

For purely speculative purposes, there are questions pertaining to the logistics surrounding a banquet of such magnitude that will accommodate several billion people in attendance. The Bible does not address the extraneous details relating to the heavenly banquet, the "marriage feast of the Lamb." We can only employ conjecture on a subject such as this and muse about what it will feel like to be a part of such a magnificent event. Will the feast be held in multiple areas within the new heavens and the new earth? We could speculate as well on who will serve the food. Will it be representatives of God's people from every generation during the human age? Will the innumerable angels get tagged for this duty? If so, how many angels will be required to serve the food, and just how much food, for that matter, will be required to feed billions of guests?

We could ponder how the menu will be decided and how many cooks will be needed to prepare the hors d'oeuvres, not to mention an unfathomable meal featuring perhaps multiple courses! Who will be doing all the cooking? How many tables and sittings will be required, and who might we sit next to? Can you foresee yourself elbowing Moses or passing Peter a plate of bread? What if Mary Magdalene were seated close enough for us to strike up a captivating conversation with her? Imagine the incredible stories concerning Jesus she could relay that are not recorded in the Bible! How about the prospect of being asked by Daniel to say the blessing or by Paul to share a devotional? Then there's the question of who will be responsible to do the clean-up. And just how sizable will the area need to be in order for everything to be stored? The future heavenly banquet holds much in the way of mystery and fascination for us.

In the Bible, the kingdom of God is often pictured as a feast or a banquet where jubilant celebration marks the end of the age of humanity and the triumph of God over His enemies. Death, sickness, and sorrow no longer hover over those at the table in the final state. Eternal bliss and blessings in the presence of God now replace the former earthly realities. The prophet Isaiah foresaw God's final judgment of all the powers that are opposed to Him in the heavens and on earth and when He will victoriously reign over His redeemed people of all ages (Isaiah 24:21–23). One of the earliest references in Scripture to an eschatological or messianic banquet also comes from Isaiah (25:6–8). There, the prophet regards the feast as an inauguration of the reign of Israel's God with an invitation to all nations to come and commune with the one true God in His abode (Zion). The veil of religious ignorance and unbelief is removed from peoples from nations far and wide. In addition, the finest of drink and food characterize the rich bounty that will accompany the event, imagery that's repeated later in Isaiah 55:1–2, where all are invited to freely share in the heritage of the servants who belong to God. For the prophet, then, the feast depicts the covenant promises of Yahweh that become covenant realities in their fullest sense for all peoples.

Other references anticipating the hope of an eschatological celebration in keeping with a festive theme and banquet-like setting are found in Isaiah 30:29 and Ezekiel 39:17–20. In fact, Israel's restoration is connected with imagery of God providing for His people (Isaiah 40:11, 49:10, 58:14; Jeremiah 50:19; Micah 5:4, 7:14). This concept is present in other texts where restoration is linked to God providing Israel with an abundance of grain and wine (Isaiah 23:18, 62:8; Jeremiah 31:10–14; Ezekiel 36:29; Joel 2:19; 2 Baruch 29:3–30:1). In Ezekiel and 1 Enoch those in the renewed Jerusalem are to eat fruit from trees evoking imagery of the tree of life in the Garden of Eden (Ezekiel 47:12; 1 Enoch 25:4–5).

In the New Testament, the Old Testament's eschatological imagery of a banquet given by God at the end of days is described as a wedding feast. John's vision of Christ in his Gospel borrows from Isaiah 62 and 63, which describe the restoration of Israel in terms of a marriage. In Luke's Gospel, Jesus's parable of the great banquet envisages a master giving a feast to which the initial invitees decline their invitation. The master's servant is then sent to other individuals who wouldn't expect to be invited to take the place of those who refuse to come to the banquet (see Luke 14:15–24, 13:29).

By contrast, the parable of the marriage banquet in Matthew's Gospel pictures a more dramatic outcome. The host-king's servants are murdered by those originally invited to his banquet, causing him to take retribution on the ones responsible. In addition, an individual found at the banquet without wedding clothes on is thrown out into the darkness (Matthew 22:1–14). In both parables (the great banquet and the marriage banquet), Jesus communicated that people who are reputed to be socially disadvantaged and deemed outcasts (e.g. the poor, the infirm, Gentiles) are invited to the banquet feast in order to fill out the places at the host's table. They too are a part of God's salvation plan and scope, a reality that was largely antithetical to the ideas and beliefs that abounded in Israel at that time. In both banquet parables, the host is seen as socially benevolent and inclusive, and the initial invitees as ungrateful.

A reference to a future heavenly banquet also occurs in the parable of the ten virgins. The overriding theme of this particular parable is the necessity of the virgins to be prepared for the coming of their bridegroom.

Those who are ready go directly into the wedding banquet, while those who are not are shut out (Matthew 25:1–13).

The Bible narrative begins with Adam being united to Eve and ends with the bride of Christ united with her groom (Jesus Christ). In Scripture, the future wedding feast that will take place in heaven suggests eternal satisfaction in the presence of God at His table. At the end of the biblical story when God's redemptive work is complete, the curtain on earthly human history will come down to the sounds of a celebratory wedding banquet. The groom will take His honoured place at the head of the table surrounded by His grateful and perfected bride—the church (see Revelation 19:7–9, 21, 22).

Feasting and a wedding supper are a recurring theme related to eschatological events and the coming messianic era. Jewish hope and Christian hope are synchronized in prophecies across Scripture of this future celebratory event. God promises a splendid banquet after He destroys death and wipes away the tears and shame of His covenant people. Is it any wonder why the Bible exhorts the saints of God to persevere (see Revelation 14:13, 16:15, 20:6, 22:7, 14)?

This book explores the theological and eternal significance of the parable of the great banquet in Luke 14 for a weary world in much need of God's truth and grace. It explores the identity of both those who are deemed worthy to attend the banquet and those whose rejection of the servant's invitation deem them unworthy to attend the eschatological feast. Several questions are addressed: How does one qualify for entrance into the great future banquet? Why do some refuse to attend the banquet? What will happen to those who remain in a state of indifference towards the banquet or who refuse to RSVP? Is there any hope for them to ever be able to attend the banquet?

People are saved by responding to God's gracious invitation to salvation through faith in His Son Jesus Christ and not by their own effort, religiosity, or heritage—as many of the religious leaders of Israel had believed. Being a microcosmic picture of salvation history, Jesus's teaching in the parable of the great banquet stresses the host's (God's) desire and readiness to fill His banquet table. The parable contrasts those individuals who from their perceived stance of self-worthiness (Israel) spurn God's invitation (they have other more interesting and important things to do) with those from a culturally unworthy social status (the unclean and Gentiles) who'd be surprised to even receive such an invitation. Therefore, we can see in the words of the parable of the great banquet an allusion to the larger eschatological dimension of the final judgment and the new order that is Jesus's kingdom, which reverses our present human, worldly order—the self-exalted being humbled and the humble being exalted.

The parable's teaching doesn't merely convey where God stands with sinners (i.e. that they're loved by Him and invited to experience Him in heaven for eternity); it also challenges sinners to consider where *they* stand with Him. The parable establishes that regardless of one's race, social status, and geographical residence, an opportunity exists for all to either respond favourably to God's invitation to salvation through His Son Jesus Christ or refuse the invitation. Of great eternal importance, the parable of the great banquet intimates that those displaying an outward righteousness and religiosity who appear as though they're primed for attending the marriage feast of the Lamb could very well fall short of reserving their place at the banquet. Moreover, the parable agrees with the entirety of Scripture in that they will not get another chance (in eternity) to change their decision should they reject God's Son before their physical death. The doors to heaven's banquet room remain wide open, but only for a limited time. *Today* is the day (age) of divine grace and opportunity to trust in God's Son; however, like any day, this one will not last forever (see 2 Peter 3:8–10).

In the book's opening chapter, I discuss the social setting of the parable and that an event such as a banquet delineated the varying degrees of status among its attendees and further determined their placement on society's totem pole of human significance. From there I present some of the different theological interpretations of Jesus's parable of the great banquet. Then the focus turns to the topic of Jesus's storytelling ability; specifically, how He was able to powerfully bridge culture with the spiritual truths of His kingdom through the use of simple and common short stories (parables) about everyday life that were relevant to His audience.

Chapter 4 presents the context of the parable. The next chapter examines the Pharisees. I highlight Israel's religious leaders' often hostile treatment—even outright rejection—of Jesus and their skeptical appraisal of His teachings (including the parable of the great banquet).

Chapters 6 to 8 cover the Lord's warnings to Israel's various religious sects and authorities as a whole. Much discussion is given to how the nation's leaders were falling short in their spiritual leadership of God's people and, consequently, were in danger of falling short of securing eternal life. Due to Israel's predominant failure to recognize Jesus of Nazareth as their nation's long-awaited and promised redeemer, a large portion of the book describes Israel's history of rebelliousness towards God and their current spiritual position.

God's steadfast and unshakable redemptive plan is discussed in chapters 9, 10 and 11. This redemptive plan includes those within Israel who were socially ostracized and people within the Gentile nations. The church also has a role in God's plan.

The final chapters of the book discuss the realities of rejection and suffering inherent in being an ambassador for Christ and the obstacles the church faces as it strives to fulfill the Great Commission in the twenty-first century.

At the end of this present earth age—after all the enemies of Christ have been defeated and the unbelieving judged and their eternal destiny assigned, and after the righteous receive their kingdom dividends for their earthly service to God—a great banquet in heaven will commence. Although we cannot know with any certainty how the event will play out, we *can* know what manner of persons will be present at the banquet dining with the Lamb of God: *His bride: the church, and all other believers whom the Father has reckoned as righteous in His Son throughout the ages.* God is throwing an end-of-days bash in His banquet hall. The size of the event will be determined by the number of people who will attend from every corner of the earth (Luke 13:29). Judging from the parable of the great banquet, no chair can be left unfilled.

CHAPTER ONE

AN RSVP WORTH RESPONDING TO
(LUKE 14:15–24)

One of my all-time favourite movies is the 1968 flick *The Party*. It starred one of the funniest men the movie industry has ever known: Peter Sellers. The comedic genius of the late actor was his innate ability to get his audience to believe in the absolute absurdity of his characters. Those familiar with Sellers's insufferable character in the Pink Panther series of movies are aware of how his acting brilliance could shed a hysterical light on any given situation—even when it wasn't warranted!

In *The Party*, Sellers played a man named Hrundi V. Bakshi, an aspiring actor who does nothing but destroy every movie set he ever steps foot on. After Bakshi mistakenly receives an invitation to an upscale party in the Hollywood Hills, he sheepishly shows up at the event and, true to his invariably klutzy form, proceeds to make the same disastrous mess of the host's home that has made him the stimulus of many a movie director's vexation. If you've seen the movie you know that near its end the home is turned into a giant pool of suds and bubbles—which not only dampens the mood of the prestigious event but hastens its merciful end.

INVITATIONS

Unlike the unfortunate (or perhaps fortunate) Hrundi V. Bakshi, it's great to be *intentionally* invited to an event. In fact, one of the finer joys in life is receiving an invitation for a party, wedding, or some other social function. Receiving an invitation to a particular event sometimes depends on who we are. Glamorous parties, socials, and banquets are often exhibitions of the who's who of society and popular culture. Celebrities, for instance, are often put on VIP lists for private parties; their name and fame precede them. When it comes to scoring an invite to highfalutin events, their position, power, and pedigree can certainly work in their favour.

At other times, it's all about who we know. I remember attending a distinguished fundraising event some years ago and getting to meet a popular professional hockey player from the Toronto Maple Leafs. Because I knew the right people, I was able to rub shoulders with celebrities and other known personalities I would normally never dream of being in the same room with. There were many in the first century who got to enjoy that very privilege with none other than God-incarnate Himself!

FEASTS AND BANQUETS IN JESUS'S DAY

Feasts and banquets were big deals to people in the ancient Near East and included much ritual, pomp, food, and wine.[1] Guests were usually welcomed by the host with a kiss, and their feet and hands were washed by servants due to the dusty terrain they travelled to reach their destination. Sometimes a guest's head, feet, beard, *and* clothes were anointed with oil before the event began. The most honoured guests received larger portions of food or more choice ones than the other guests. Often the feasts and banquets were enlivened by entertainment that featured singing, different forms of music, dance, and even riddles. A banquet of great size was known to last as long as a week or more.

Banquets and elaborate fetes in our Lord's day were usually held in honour of notable persons or as a means of celebrating certain events. Anything from ordinary meals to birthday celebrations to wedding feasts, funerals, and elaborate banquets were among the most important settings in which shame and honour within society were magnified.

---

[1] Dennis Smith, "Meal Customs (Greco-Roman)," in *Anchor Bible Dictionary*, vol. 4, ed. David Noel Freedman (New York: Doubleday, 1992), 651.

The religious feasts prescribed in the Mosaic Law in the Old Testament were a significant part of the social fabric of Israel. Such feasts, in Jesus's day, irrespective of their focus, could reflect where one stood within society's pecking order. The who's who of Israel could not only be spotted at such events but be found occupying the best seats! If you were an esteemed individual this meant you were assured a seat of honour at the table by the host. Conversely, if you were deemed a scoundrel, were untrustworthy, or were of some bearably tolerable ilk, you were assigned a less desirable seat at the table. Worse still, if you were considered somewhat of an outcast or were an unclean person, the bleacher seats were always an option—which meant you had to sit alone somewhere within the periphery of the other guests. If you were *never* invited to a party, well … you basically didn't matter very much. Such public gatherings highlighted the neediness of the physically and socially challenged among them. These persons were tolerated, not celebrated.

It was a society of profound social distinction. Guests at banquets were seated according to their respective rank. Therefore, each position at the table had a value assigned to it, making the feast-setting an opportune place to advance one's status.[2] Such was the sociocultural backdrop draped behind the stage Jesus set for the actors in His kingdom-invitation drama, the parable of the great banquet in Luke 14.

For the audience of Luke's Gospel, the communal meal was connected to worship. Believers participated in a feast that surrounded the early church's observance of the Eucharist (the Lord's Supper). In the parable of the great banquet, Jesus links the believer's worshipful entrance into God's presence and the heavenly eternal state with a celebratory feast. The parable repeats and expands the theme of hospitality Jesus stresses to the Pharisee whose feast He is attending. The Saviour points out that not only are some at the feast amateurishly jockeying for the most distinguished seats in the house but, also, people who should've been invited were not. The Lord proceeds to teach that those who *should* be the first to go into the messianic feast in the last day are excusing themselves from it, making room for other more marginal folks, people whom most Jews gasped at the thought of God allowing into His kingdom, and ahead of many of them!

[2] Smith, "Meal Customs," 651–52.

Jesus has a lot to say through the parable of the great banquet for everyone who either knows Him as Lord, rejects Him as such, or sees Him as an inferior religious figure in history. Despite the dichotomous issues that exist between Jews and Christians culturally and theologically, people of both faiths rightfully anticipate a future heavenly banquet to commence with their places secured in it. The question, then, is not whether there *will* be a banquet but who among those two groups will actually *make* it in. Then there's the matter that those who have not heard about the banquet or the God of the banquet need to be invited!

CHAPTER

TWO

INTERPRETING THE PARABLE OF THE GREAT BANQUET

One can interpret much of Scripture to accommodate a particular worldview or theological leaning. Instead of drawing out the intended meaning of a passage or teaching (the discipline of exegesis), some people make the mistake of reading into or imposing their own interpretation upon the text. I've yet to meet anyone who doesn't want to be right about what the Bible teaches. Yet we can't always equate what we believe is "right" with what is actually *correct.* Interpreting Scripture is certainly not the same thing as reading, knowing, and even believing what it says. If our interpretation of Scripture is incorrect, the fact that we've read it will make little difference in our lives.

Have you ever listened to a song and wondered what the songwriter was really saying? Sometimes we hear certain lyrics incorrectly and therefore sing them as such. Some lyrics are so veiled and abstruse it's almost impossible to decipher the song's meaning. If you're like me, you like to comprehend the true intent and message behind a songwriter's lyrics. In fact, obscure and cryptic lyrics can actually devalue a song's meaning and poignancy when they're misinterpreted. Whether they're spoken, written, or sung, words communicate something to us. The words we want to be *absolutely* certain we're interpreting correctly are the ones authored by God in *His* Word!

Thankfully, interpreting Jesus's parables isn't quite as onerous a task as decoding certain song lyrics!

Although God speaks to be understood, some who heard Jesus failed to possess the necessary spiritual ears to grasp the truth He was disclosing. Hearing God's Word is one thing; comprehending it is quite another! Fact is, understanding the theological meaning of Jesus's parables can lead to much interpretative speculation.

NOTED INTERPRETATIONS OF THE PARABLE OF THE GREAT BANQUET

As is the case with all of Jesus's parables, there are numerous interpretations of the parable of the great banquet. The parable has been interpreted as reflecting the doctrine of election (in terms of God's choosing of those whom He desires to save), as being a corrective rebuke on attitudes towards the rich and poor, and as being further justification for the continuation of the Great Commission and world missions in the church (to include the evangelization of Jews). The parable has also been interpreted as being an anti-Semitic statement by implying that Israel has been rejected by its God.[3]

Interpretation depends in part on where one perceives the parable to end. For example, if the parable of the great banquet ends at verse 21, then Luke's familiar use of the reversal to announce the gospel is the format here: insiders are out and outsiders are in. If the parable proper extends through verse 23, then it is almost inevitable that one thinks of God's offer first to the rejected and the marginal in Israel (on the streets of the city) and then to Gentiles (strangers on the outskirts of the city).[4]

Of importance to note is that Matthew and Luke render their feast-oriented parables differently in their respective Gospels. In Matthew's account of the parable of the marriage banquet there are three sendings of servants to the original guests, two excuses offered for the refusal, along with one sending of the king's army to destroy those who killed his servants, followed by the final sending of even more servants to the

[3] See a brief refutation of this argument in Craig A. Evans, *Luke*, New International Biblical Commentary (Peabody: Hendrickson Publishers, 1990), 227.

[4] Fred B. Craddock, *Luke*, Interpretation: A Bible Commentary for Teaching and Preaching (Louisville: John Knox Press, 1990), 179–80.

substitute invitees (see Matthew 22:1–14). By contrast, Luke has only one sending of a servant (singular) to the original guests and three excuses as to why they cannot attend the banquet, followed by two sendings to substitute guests.

In Matthew, the host is a king and the feast is specifically held in celebration of a wedding banquet for a son. Conversely, Luke's host is a "certain man" who prepares a "great" banquet, not a wedding feast per se. Matthew's account mentions the host-king's inspection of a guest who was "not wearing wedding clothes," who is subsequently bound and tossed out into the "darkness" (an expression depicting severe punishment). As well, Matthew's parable of the wedding banquet concludes with the statement "For many are invited, but few are chosen" (Matthew 22:14). Luke, on the other hand, describes the substitute guests as being "the poor, the crippled, the blind, and the lame" (14:21). However, like Matthew, Luke also ends his recording of Jesus's parable on an ominous tone: "I tell you, not one of those who were invited will get a taste of my banquet" (14:24).

What should we make of the similarities and differences between the two Gospel accounts of Jesus's parables of the marriage banquet (in Matthew) and the great banquet (in Luke)?

When interpreting passages in the Gospels, it's helpful to keep in mind that each author had his own particular kingdom agenda to communicate when writing and sought to present a particular facet of the Saviour.

If Matthew was mostly concerned with the quality of Israel's religious leaders (for he placed the parable of the wedding banquet among a series of other parables dealing with that issue) and, by comparison, Luke was concerned with showcasing God's inclusion of the downtrodden and Gentiles into His kingdom, as well as the state of the religious leadership within Israel (albeit not as directly), what common points exist between these fraternal-twin parables?

We can rest assured that the Gospel writers heard Jesus correctly on both occasions. The Lord chose the players and plotlines of His teaching stories intentionally, depending on the audience hearing His message and the corresponding point He strove to make *to* that particular audience.

The Lord appeared to have had two fundamental objectives in mind for teaching this specific parable of the great banquet when and where He did. First, there was erroneous teaching and popular beliefs about who was fit for the kingdom of heaven and who was not. That needed clarification. Secondly, Jesus's parable seems to emphasize the point that the invitation to enter God's kingdom, which was spurned by one group (the self-righteous and unbelieving Jews), has been freely extended to other groups of people who were thought to be ill-suited to inherit the blessing of heaven (the physically and spiritually destitute and every manner of Gentile). In the following chapters, we explore these objectives along with the spiritual and eternal ramifications inherent within Jesus's parable of the great banquet in Luke 14, a parable that carries as much significance for the believer in Christ today as it does for the unsaved.

REFLECTIVE QUESTIONS

1. What is your personal method for studying the Bible so as to properly interpret and understand its content, teachings, and applications?
2. What are your thoughts on some of the noted interpretations of the parable of the great banquet?
3. Are there any other interpretations or applications of the parable you can come up with that align with the Bible's teachings?
4. Which of the two feast/banquet-oriented parables (in Luke 14 and Matthew 22) is more effective for its teaching on the kingdom of God? If you say they are both effective, choose a few elements from each that stand out to you.
5. In your opinion, do most of the sermons you hear today contextualize the biblical content being taught (by mentioning the events of surrounding passages) and impart it in a way that connects the historical distance (original circumstances, cultural atmosphere) to the realities of the 21st century world and current-day issues affecting those who are listening?

CHAPTER

THREE

PARABLES—COMMUNICATING TRUTH THROUGH STORY

The Gospels contain accounts where Jesus uses a peculiar style of teaching that conveys truths pertaining to the kingdom of God. The original audience knew there was more to the simplicity of these stories than immediately apparent. The parables had a ring of cultural familiarity to them. They were concise in length and contained a deep meaning. They were spoken in such a manner that the people hearing them were left either shrugging their shoulders or eager for more. The Lord's parables made believers out of some who had possessed a benumbed indifference towards Him. Conversely, some people chose to crystallize their unbelief. On occasion, the parables offended some who solved the not-so-veiled puzzle. The Gospel accounts also reveal how Jesus's storytelling prowess baptized still another crop of listeners (the Pharisees) in the indignant waters of their self-righteousness. Most within this particular crowd were clearly ungrateful for Jesus and spurned Him just to save their spiritual faces.

Far from rhapsodizing about the powerful beauty of His salvation message, Jesus frames these teachings into stories packed with challenging intent and spirit-shaping content. Such stories were not entirely safe to hear, and neither could they have been dismissed as tired "heard-before" grumblings, the kind that came from rabbis perched upon their soapbox pulpits. Yet the question remains as to how such relatively short stories could grab the conscience and force one to think so long and hard.

Truth is, great stories *and* storytellers accomplish such ends.

I am a lover of great stories, perhaps like yourself. As someone who enjoys reading autobiographies and researching information, I appreciate engaging stories, especially those that penetrate the heart and cause the reader to do a little introspection. The story could be a tale and involve a mouse or a hobbit's house; it could involve history or ministry. Whether they're fictional or of the "real-life" variety, stories—even simple ones—help to colour in some of the black and white perceptions and understandings we have of people and life in general.

There's nothing like a story to enlarge insight, stir thoughts, and motivate our actions. Even a nondescript story can be masterfully transformed into a memorable, touching, and even educative experience when put into the hands of a compelling storyteller. Great storytellers have a knack for communicating a story in a manner that evokes the sorts of thoughts, emotions, and responses they desire to draw out of their listeners.

Klyne R. Snodgrass states, "Stories are one of the few places that allow us to see reality, at least the reality the author creates. There, to a degree we cannot do in real life, we can discern motives, keep score, know who won, and what success and failure look like."[5]

A parable, in a general sense, *is* a story—albeit a very compact one. We needn't wade through a gamut of paragraphs, plots, chapters, and characters in order to digest a parable. A parable, in fact, doesn't give us the *whole* story concerning the story it tells. Parables, by nature, lead us to a destination but often challenge us to imagine possibilities along the way.

STORIES FROM THE MASTER STORYTELLER IN THE GOSPELS

Jesus's parables are stories based on human needs that contain "kingdom" agendas and lessons. They generally consist of two levels: the *story* level (which appeals and relates to a common experience) and the *truth* level

[5] Klyne Snodgrass, *Stories with Intent: A Comprehensive Guide to the Parables of Jesus*, 2nd ed. (Grand Rapids: Eerdmans, 2018), 1.

(the spiritual reality behind the story). In their basic makeup, Jesus's parables aim to awaken spiritual understanding, prod the conscience, and move people to righteous action.

Jesus excelled when it came to the art of storytelling and communicating in general—especially as one who taught with unequalled authority and wisdom (Matthew 7:28–29). This explains why the Lord could be spellbinding and effective in conveying spiritual truth within the context of a simple story.

Jesus linked everyday life scenarios within His culture to spiritual realities. He did this to illustrate truths, punctuate principles relating to the kingdom of God, and, ultimately, to influence lives. Whenever the Saviour taught in parabolic form it was done for the purpose of *weeding out* the crowds following Him. He used parables to separate those who were decidedly deaf to God's call from those whose spiritual ears remained attuned to His teachings. Simply, the parables of Jesus functioned as a means to elicit a reply from those whom the parable's underlying spiritual truth was meant to impact.

Parables were "told to address and capture the hearers, to bring them up short about their own actions, or to cause them to respond in some way to Jesus and His ministry."[6] In one sense, the Lord taught in parables so that those around Him who lacked spiritual understanding would actually *remain* in that condition.

Jesus put it like this:

> "[The disciples] are permitted to understand the secrets of the Kingdom of Heaven, but others are not. To those who listen to my teaching, more understanding will be given … But for those who are not listening, even what little understanding they have will be taken away from them. This is why I use these parables, For they look, but they don't really see. They hear, but they don't really listen or understand." (Matthew 13:11–13, NLT)

Jesus knew that true, keen, and learned students would seek clarification from their teacher. Therefore, the Lord's parables worked to expose any individuals who had a genuine interest in what He had to say and had blended in among the throngs of people following Him. Jesus's

---

[6] Gordon D. Fee and Douglas Stuart, *How to Read the Bible for All Its Worth*, 4th ed. (Grand Rapids: Zondervan, 2003), 138.

parables also possess an element of secrecy that He intended to exclusively make known to those who were among His disciples (Luke 8:10).

The Lord is all business when it comes to imparting life-and-death spiritual truth. Jesus appears to have no interest in merely scoring retinues of roadies for His evangelistic tours. He teaches not just for the sake of attracting listeners but for the ultimate purpose of redeeming and changing the lives of those whom His heavenly Father has given Him. The Saviour of the world doesn't pander to the hysteria and robust fanfare that shadow His ministry. He doesn't seek followers who follow Him for the superficial pleasure of hanging out with someone as audacious and compelling as He is. The Lord desires followers who are interested in spiritual *truth*—specifically, the truth embodied in *Him* as the heaven-sent Lamb of God.

REFLECTIVE QUESTIONS

1. Were you read stories at bedtime as a child?
2. How often do you read stories of "everyday" people in the newspapers or on the internet?
3. What were some of the factors that made Jesus such an amazing storyteller for His time?
4. What is your favourite parable of Jesus's and why?
5. What parable/s do you find difficult to understand and why?
6. How would you explain why some people gravitated closer to the Lord on account of His parables, while others lost interest in or pulled away from Him altogether?
7. Can you find parallels between the teachings in Jesus's parables and His greater body of teachings throughout the Gospels?
8. Do you feel storytelling is as valued in our culture as it was in Jesus's day? Why or why not?

CHAPTER FOUR

THE CONTEXT OF THE PARABLE OF THE GREAT BANQUET

All you had to do was stick close to Jesus Christ and you were sure to hear a provocative zinger fly out of Him! Various accounts within the Gospels place the Lord in a scrum-like setting where fans and haters alike—as if holding a recording device in front of Him—ask Him to comment on the latest religiopolitical firestorm.

Israel's religious leaders likely spent many a day and night being royally miffed at the Saviour for something He said about them. The Pharisees were often the bullseye Jesus was aiming at with His teaching; and the truth He communicated was often too inconvenient for them to handle! While some religious leaders were either convicted or left standing amid a fog of misunderstanding, it is clear that others were not impressed and compensated for it.

A rather fascinating dimension to Jesus's ministry was His reading of and response to people, situations, and environments. Often when the Saviour was asked a question or when someone made a comment in regard to His teaching, Jesus responded by taking into consideration the immediate physical surroundings from which the inquiry or statement sprung (for example, see Matthew 24:1–2). Whether the Lord was standing amid the farmlands or walking on the surface of seawater, whether He was casting lines with fishermen or attending a tax collector's (or even a Pharisee's) soiree, Jesus could potter a spiritual lesson from the clay of any context He was situated in.

When the context of their conversation with Him featured the religious leaders' insistence that they were wholly capable of leading God's people, Jesus responded by upending their cart of self-accreditation—and then some. The Lord used such incendiary and even ghastly terms as "blind," "child of hell," "whitewashed tombs," and "brood of vipers" to describe members of the Pharisees and the other religious leaders (see Matthew 15:14, 23:15, 27, 33). Talk about provocative quotes!

When the conversation's context surrounded the Pharisees' criticisms of His disciples' "unlawful" actions on the Sabbath, Jesus retorted by calling Himself "Lord of the Sabbath," while educating the Pharisees that on the holiest of days, God wills that "good" deeds trump "sacrifice"—in short, that the Sabbath day was made for the *people*, not the other way around. When the context revolved around the Pharisees' convenient exaltation of Abraham, Jesus's newsflash to members of the sect was that He (the Lord) actually *predates* the patriarch by an eternal margin (see John 8:58)! No wonder the religious leaders scurried to intentionally misquote Jesus, to take His statements so grossly out of their context. The realization that they were losing badly to Him in the coveted polls of propaganda *and* popularity was setting in. They played chicken with the Almighty and predictably blinked!

JESUS: POPULAR AND CONTROVERSIAL

It is human nature to want to see people who we believe are breaking the law be caught and convicted. It's quite acceptable to feel upset, even righteously angry, when we feel justice is not being served and when we perceive that someone is getting away with lawlessness. I imagine that's how the Pharisees must have felt whenever they witnessed Jesus do or say something that didn't follow their interpretation of the Mosaic Law or when Jesus's claims to divinity crossed over into the realm of blasphemy. One way the frustrated leaders of Israel's religious establishment sought to remedy the problem was to corner Jesus in the hope that He might mess up and prove Himself to be the phony hero and lawbreaker they believed Him to be.

The Gospels impress upon us that Jesus was both widely and wildly popular in His day. In fact, some twenty-one centuries after the Lord took His first earthly breath as a heaven-come-down newborn and then grew to eventually blow away the collective mind of humanity, He is more popular than ever. His divine highlight reel of signs and wonders has been preached everywhere from the pulpits of grand cathedrals to the most cramped of underground churches. Even those who reviled the Lord were largely motivated by His popularity.

The term *popularity*, when applied to a person, can take on varying shades of meaning and consequence depending on who you talk to. Case in point, all one had to do was say the names Donald Trump and Hillary Clinton during their respective runs for the White House and, immediately, a can of ultra-opinionated and colourful worms would be opened.

The same could be said of the Son of God during His earthly ministry years.

Jesus Christ will always be one of the most polarizing figures to walk our planet. Despite being the people's rabbi, the Lord received mixed reviews within the court of Israel's religious leaders' opinions. Depending on who was chiming in, the Saviour was thought to be "a good man," "the Prophet," "the Messiah," one who "deceives," and even "demon-possessed" (John 7:12–41). Even the temple guards who were sent by the religious leaders to arrest Jesus at the Feast of Tabernacles were mesmerized by Him and declined to seize the Lord. The guards went one step further by declaring in the presence of the chief priests and Pharisees, "No one ever spoke the way this man does" (John 7:45–46).

Jesus was the proverbial "toast of the town" almost as much as He was alleged to have made the most-wanted list for crimes committed against the Mosaic Law. The Lord was as favoured as He was doubted and was followed almost as much as He was overlooked and discarded. Oppositional forces of confrontation and indignation slammed Him even as open acts of adoration and celebration from supporters exalted Him.

The Son of God was always in demand, always under the lights of His culture's insatiable hounding and stake in Him. John's Gospel records how an inquisitive Pharisee named Nicodemus amiably approached Jesus at night, likely out of a fear of being criticized by fellow members of the sect. The high-ranking and high-road-taking Nicodemus seemed to intimate that at least some of those among the Pharisees actually *believed* Jesus was sent of God (John 3:2). Joseph of Arimathea, another individual associated with the leadership of Israel (a member of the Sanhedrin and likely a Pharisee as well), became a follower of Jesus and claimed His body after the crucifixion in order to bury it in his tomb. And how could we overlook the moderate Pharisee named Gamaliel who during the early stages of the church's expansion also kept an open mind to Jesus and His gospel (see Acts 5:33–39)? These heartening realities aside, the Gospel writers communicate that the majority of the religious elite within Israel refused to follow Jesus.

The one thing that was synonymous with Jesus's popularity was *controversy*, and controversy always attracts attention and speculation. In Jesus's case, His controversial ministry attracted, among other things, the worst slander, surreptitious activity, and covert enemies.

As author W. Phillip Keller described,

> Wherever [Jesus] went He was followed. If not by the general masses, then by the persistent Pharisees and Sadducees: Veritable bloodhounds that would not relent, they trailed and tracked Him everywhere with cruel, crafty cunning. These deadly intelligentsia were forever demanding, insisting that somehow Jesus should supply them with some "sign" that He was in truth the Son of God … they wanted empirical proof that He was deity.[7]

Every authoritative stripe among Israel's religious superintendency worked overtime to get Jesus to submit to their investigations concerning His claims to divinity. Luke 14 records Jesus sidestepping one of their clandestinely conceived landmines embedded by a batch of His antagonizing rivals. Luke tells us that the meal hosted by the prominent Pharisee was held on the Sabbath day (Luke 14:1). The Sabbath was sacrosanct in that it was a day the Law stipulated was to be set aside for reflecting on the glory of God (see Deuteronomy 5:12–15). It also happened to be the one day of the week when Jesus seemed to ruffle the holier-than-thou feathers of the Pharisees the most. Simply put, the Sabbath was a time when Jesus's interactions with His detractors were at their most tempestuous.

[7] W. Phillip Keller, *Rabboni: Which Is to Say, Master*, 2nd ed. (Grand Rapids: Kregel Publications, 1997), 157.

IT'S A SET-UP: RESCUING AND HEALING ON THE SABBATH

In Luke 14:2, the Lord is seated within intimate proximity of a man who's been suffering from a painful physical condition that is likely dropsy (the retention of fluid affecting parts of the body). That this infirm person is even at the meal and then placed in front of Jesus in the seating arrangement suggests that something cagey is afoot. Given the Pharisees' track record of resorting to skulduggery where the Saviour is concerned, it's possible that the host of the event—along with any other conspiring minds present—desires to trap Jesus in a situation where He'll have to heal the suffering fellow on the Sabbath, an action that the Pharisees consider unlawful "work." No wonder Luke makes a point of noting that Jesus is being "carefully watched" by His detractors (Luke 14:1; Mark 3 records Jesus as being in a similar situation while worshipping in the synagogue).

Previously in Luke's Gospel, the Pharisees also endeavour to entrap Jesus (11:53–54). Clearly, there are those among the sect who seek to bring Him down.[8] Being the prime ringleaders in the "Never Jesus" movement, the Pharisees are using their numerous failures to terminate His ministry as motivation for catching a red-handed Jesus finally doing something—anything—that will inconvertibly convict Him of being a lawbreaker.

The Gospel narratives, however, show a divinely forewarned and forearmed Jesus continuously tripping up the Pharisees' best laid plans to get the better of Him. The Lord will not let the contingent of colluders in His midst off the hook of His accountability. They poked the Lion of Judah, and now they'll hear the sound of His righteous roar. For starters, Jesus poses a question to the crowd at the feast: "Is it lawful to heal on the Sabbath or not?" (Luke 14:3). Notice here that the Lord isn't asking if *work* is permitted on the Sabbath but rather if *healing* is.

Cue the proverbial sound of a pin dropping in an otherwise deathly silent room. No one is willing to give a response to the moral gauntlet the Saviour has just thrown down by asking a question that has only one possible answer. There is neither a flicker of mercy nor a pinch of compassion to be found among the feast's attendees for the plight of the infirm man in their company. Rabbis, as part of their man-made regulations, prohibit healing on the Sabbath unless it is feared that the infirm person could die the next day. Nonetheless, if "love" is to do "no

---

[8] Evans, *Luke*, 218, states the sick man was a plant to test Jesus.

harm to a neighbor," then the Pharisees who preside over the Law are the ones especially guilty this day of *breaking* the Law (Romans 13:10; see Leviticus 19:18)!

The Lord surveys the hearts of those assembled around the room, an observation that undoubtedly leaves Him deeply grieved and angry. Unlike humans, God is able to get angry by the right amount, at the right time, at the right people, and for the right reasons. He always responds righteously whenever He is angered. The same proves to be true of our Lord whenever He is put on the spot, as is the case when He attends the esteemed Pharisee's dinner party.

Jesus proceeds to touch the dropsy-inflicted man in front of Him (an offensive act to Jews all on its own) and heal him. After the healing takes place, the Lord promptly sends "him on his way" (Luke 14:4). Perhaps Jesus wants to spare the man from having to remain at a gathering that he (as well as the Saviour) may have been invited to under false pretenses.

In true rabbi fashion, the Lord volleys a subsequent question into the guests' court relating to lawful actions on the Sabbath. This inquiry is designed to answer the Lord's initial question in Luke 14:3. "If one of you has a child or an ox that falls into a well on the Sabbath day, will you not immediately pull him out?" (Luke 14:5).

The question hovers over the room like an ominous zeppelin waiting to crush the feast's attendees in their apparent ignorance. The fact that Jesus questions the Pharisees and "experts" of the law *before* the healing takes place makes it hard for them to pull any protests afterwards. If it were a game of chess Jesus could victoriously exclaim, "Checkmate!"

Like Jesus's first question in Luke 14:3, His second one in Luke 14:5 has only one possible and acceptable answer.

Whether it was out of embarrassment, fear, or even conviction, the mouths of the guests present at the Pharisee's home had been sewn shut; once again they offered no counter to Jesus's subsequent query. Luke writes that the Pharisees and experts in the law "had nothing to say" in reply (Luke 14:6). The Lord had broadsided his audience—and the host Pharisee probably wished he hadn't bothered trying to corner the rabbi from Nazareth.

Importantly, "Jesus' action was 'unlawful' only according to rabbinic interpretations, not according to the Mosaic law itself."[9] Jesus challenged

[9] *The Study NIV Bible* (Grand Rapids: Zondervan, 2011), 1734.

fallacious teachings when He fulfilled to perfection the Law's requirements down to the very smallest letter in the Hebrew alphabet (see Matthew 5:18–20).

The enemies of Jesus were learning the hard way that the Lord sought neither to lower the Law's standard nor to abolish it completely. Rather, the Saviour taught that the totality and essence (or spirit) of the Law's commands and teachings found their ultimate outworking in the combination of two commandments: "'Love the Lord your God with all your heart and with all your soul and with all your mind.' This is the first and greatest commandment. And the second is like it: 'Love your neighbor as yourself.' All the Law and the Prophets hang on these two commandments" (Matthew 22:37–40).

Jesus's redeeming ministry brought the actions of rescuing animals and healing infirm persons together under one righteous roof: to do good and save life on the Sabbath (see Mark 2:23–27, 3:1–6). Our Lord knew that His hearers *would* rescue a donkey or ox that had fallen into a well on the Sabbath and therefore couldn't possibly begrudge meeting severe *human* need on the same day.

TIME FOR A PARABLE

Luke tells us that a man of keen introspection is in attendance at the meal being held at the Pharisee's home. The same man, after witnessing Jesus's healing of the dropsy-inflicted individual and hearing Him express in a parable how a guest at a party shouldn't aspire to sit in the most esteemed seats, perks up and blurts out, "Blessed is the one who will eat at the feast in the kingdom of God" (Luke 14:15). By his insightful remark, the unidentified banquet attendee proves that he grasps something many of the Pharisees fail to—that blessing and honour in the future heavenly kingdom is attained not by travelling the congested human highway of entitlement but by taking the lesser-travelled off-ramp of *humility*.

The Pharisees who were pocking the spiritual face of Israel with attitudes and platitudes slanted towards self-righteousness and self-preservation had their just deserts coming to them—Son of God style, deserts Jesus often served up in the form of bite-sized and yet hard-to-swallow parables. What better time to teach on the great banquet (the marriage feast of the Lamb) than when the context is a gathering filled with food and people?

The Lord seizes upon the idyllic moment and uses the aforementioned unidentified man's comment as a launching pad for yet another apropos parable, this one pertaining to the way in which we come into God's kingdom so that we may take our privileged place at the future marriage feast of the Lamb. In response to all the duplicitous behaviour undergirding the meal and the failure of those present to extend grace and dignity to the infirm man, Jesus takes the opportunity to teach those in His midst an enlightening value of His kingdom: God's mercy often extends far beyond the limits to which those who are most religious (e.g. the Pharisees) usually restrict it.

Jesus would have the attendees at the Pharisee's home (as well as us today) realize that to be invited to *His* banquet is to be chosen by God to enter the kingdom of heaven, an invitation based not on one's ecclesiastical pedigree, spiritual legacy, or efforts to be righteous but on the sole basis of God's *grace.* More than likely, the anti-Jesus brass among the meal's guests would correctly discern that *they* are being singled-out (if not indicted) in the Lord's latest parable!

REFLECTIVE QUESTIONS

1. From your knowledge of history, can you recall examples of religious figures who were popular yet opposed by their culture or the media? For what reasons were they criticized/opposed?
2. How could Jesus's teaching on how one enters the kingdom of God have been so counterintuitive to the understanding of the Pharisees and other Jews at the banquet?
3. What made Jesus so unique for His day, and why did the religious establishment of Israel treat Him with such contempt?
4. From surveying the Gospel accounts, what ways do you see in which the Pharisees and the other religious leaders tried to trap Jesus by using the Law's commandments? How did Jesus handle those situations?
5. Discuss the difference between the *spirit and letter* of the Law. How did Jesus fulfill the former?
6. Cite some examples in the Gospel accounts where Jesus used His immediate physical surroundings as a context for His teaching.

7. Jesus actually teaches two parables in Luke 14. How does the one (verses 8 to 11) relate to the other (verses 16 to 24)?
8. Do you feel that the silent treatment Jesus received as a response to His two convicting questions parallels how unsaved sinners may respond at His throne of judgment one day?

CHAPTER

FIVE

THE PHARISEES

One recurring theme in the Gospels is conflict. The Saviour's message hardly reflects an "I love you, you love me; I'm okay, you're okay—we're all okay" PR tour. In fact, the Gospels are festooned with the interactions and altercations Jesus had with His ever-militant detractors.

When the Lord has something on His mind, He speaks it, whether other minds are inquiring or not. Many of His comments aim to correct theology or rebuke shallow and showy spirituality. Often His comments are directed at a specific person or group. Most of the conflict Jesus experiences, however, revolves around those to whom much spiritual responsibility is entrusted— Israel's religious elite. The Lord expects such figures, who are supposed to know better, to *do* better as leaders of God's people. The Pharisees, specifically, appear to be a target for the Saviour to take aim and fire His righteous judgments at. Consequently, the Pharisees are cited in the Gospels as being the prime agitators in a campaign against Jesus.

WHO WERE THE PHARISEES?

The name *Pharisee* means "separated" or "distinguished" and is synonymous with *scribe*; they were repeatedly described as "people who transmit, preserve, and develop the tradition of the law in its written and oral form."[10] The Pharisees were a literate, organized sect that functioned as a political interest group, and though they did not have direct power, they sought influence with the governing class.[11] Josephus presents the Pharisees as the most prominent and influential group in Palestinian Jewish life and the most precise interpreters of the law.[12] They practised and interpreted the law in their own way.[13]

The Gospels present the Pharisees as opponents to Jesus. In Luke particularly, Pharisees are described as not caring for the poor and depriving them of justice because they are outside of the social order (14:1–24, 17:14, 18:9–14).[14]

The Pharisee sect was looked upon by most commoners as the authoritative interpreters of the Torah. Pharisees who practised a more liberal track of Judaism under the School of Hillel had somewhat of a missions focus to their ministry, willingly accepting Gentile converts and seeking to bring them under Mosaic Law, such as requiring adult circumcision.

But the majority of Pharisees were occupied with keeping Israel's national and religious identities and interests aligned with the commandments of the Mosaic Law that governed the spiritual, moral, and social affairs of God's people. Author Philip Yancey elaborates,

> The society was, in effect, a religious caste system based on steps toward holiness, and the Pharisees' scrupulosity reinforced the system daily. All their rules on washing hands and avoiding defilement were an attempt to make themselves acceptable to God. Had not God set forth lists of desirable (spotless) and undesirable (flawed, unclean) animals for use in sacrifice? Had not God banned sinners, menstruating women, the physically deformed, and other "undesirables" from the temple?[15]

To a degree, the Pharisees should be lauded for their painstaking intentions and efforts to ensure that Israel's theocratic rule of law was

---

[10] Eckhard Schnabel, "Pharisees," in *The New Interpreter's Dictionary of the Bible*, vol. 4, ed. Katharine Doob Sakenfeld (Nashville: Abingdon Press, 2009), 486.

[11] Anthony Saldarini, "Pharisees," in *Anchor Bible Dictionary*, vol. 5, ed. Freedman, 293.

[12] Schnabel, "Pharisees," 488.

[13] Saldarini, "Pharisees," 293.

[14] Saldarini, "Pharisees," 293.

[15] Philip Yancey, *The Jesus I Never Knew* (Grand Rapids: Zondervan, 1995), 153.

upheld. For many, their objective to maintain a righteous Israel and to obey every law meticulously was godly and noble. Like other Jewish persons, the Pharisees were quite aware of the silent treatment God gave their nation after the ministry of the prophets faded into Old Testament history. They were also cognizant of Israel's disobedience toward and discord with God and the subsequent judgments He levied on them as a result. In that regard, the Pharisees should not be faulted for trying to keep the Jewish people from transgressing against God and continuing to endure His wrath.

However, in their attempts to have their fellow Jews live God-fearing and law-abiding lives, the Pharisees felt it necessary to conjure up extraneous rules and regulations and set them as a bulwark around the parameter of the Law, an initiative designed to deter God's people from trespassing against its commands and directives. What the Pharisees fancied as a nostrum for Israel's track record of sin wound up compounding the yoke of remaining faithful to their God while living under an oppressive Roman regime!

The Gospels give us the impression that the Pharisees saw themselves as the true guardians of the Law's gate who did the thankless work of enforcing the Law's commands to keep Israel in God's favour. While they waited for the promised Messiah's coming and the subsequent redemption of their nation, the Pharisees took the responsibility (and often the credit) for being the true watchmen of Jewish spiritual affairs.

Their Messiah did, of course, arrive, in the person of Jesus—and what the Son of God saw in the Pharisees wasn't what the members of the sect were promoting themselves as being! Jesus exposed their promoting of pet regulations and man-made traditions as unnecessary for salvation. Who knew better than the Saviour that the Old Testament Law never *saved* anyone but only pointed to one's need *to* be saved—and that, by Him? Jesus accused the Pharisees of protecting the "letter" of the Law (in Fort-Knox-like fashion) at the shameless expense of overlooking and undervaluing its intended *spirit*!

Though outwardly the Pharisees were recognized as religious figures and leaders, Jesus accused them of insincerity—more authentic in their phoniness than plausible in their genuineness. The Pharisees were majoring in ethical minors while remaining spiritual minors when it came to the major stuff that mattered to God! Jesus likened their finicky approach to righteous living to people who were careful of not ingesting something as tiny as a gnat yet seemed perfectly all right with attempting to gulp down something as massive as a camel (Matthew 23:24–26).

Another unflattering knock on the character of the Pharisees from the Lord's perspective was their penchant for wanting to be seen. The Lord pointed out how the Pharisees liked the sound of their own voices during times of public prayer and revelled in any accolades they'd procure from open acts of righteousness (Matthew 6:1–5). Jesus disapproved of the Pharisees' wanting to be privileged individuals and have the most socially important and honoured seats in the synagogues and banquets they hosted and frequented. Often, the Gospels portray the sect as a troupe of shifty clerics whose religious performances had them dancing to the beat of their own self-significance, a group of know-it-alls and show-offs who made a nauseating habit of crowing about their spiritual vitality and indispensable presence within Israel.

Jesus challenges the Pharisees to measure up to the spiritually lofty pedestal they'd constructed for themselves on the backs of their fellow Israelites. The Lord uses a particular word with great ease to size up the spiritual calibre of the Pharisees—*hypocrite.* The hypocrisy of the Pharisees is "sin; failure to do God's will is concealed behind the pious appearance of outward conduct."[16] Rather than simply and unassumingly doing the will of God, the actions of the Pharisees reveal "the jarring contradiction between what they say and what they do, between the outward appearance and the inward lack of righteousness … they are concerned about their status with men rather than their standing before God. They thus fail to achieve the righteousness which they pretend to have."[17]

Is it any wonder, then, why Jesus refers to the Pharisees as hypocrites as often as He does? It is the ideal word to describe the self-awareness-lacking sect. The Gospels expose how the Pharisees intentionally failed to comply with the very towering expectations they inflicted on their fellow Jewish people (see Matthew 23:23; Luke 11:46).

[16] Ulrich Wilckens, "Ὑποκρίνομαι, Συνυποκρίνομαι, Ὑπόκρισις, Ὑποκριτής, Ἀνυπόκριτος," in *Theological Dictionary of the New Testament*, eds. Gerhard Kittel, Geoffrey W. Bromiley, and Gerhard Friedrich (Grand Rapids: Eerdmans, 1964), 567–568.
[17] Wilckens, "Ὑποκρίνομαι, Συνυποκρίνομαι, Ὑπόκρισις, Ὑποκριτής, Ἀνυπόκριτος," 567–568.

WILL THE PHARISEES ACCEPT JESUS'S INVITATION?

A brief summary of Old Testament history on the part of the Saviour reminds Israel's religious establishment that they—like their "ancestors" who "killed the prophets"—are hardly paragons of spiritual fidelity and credibility, for He knows they will one day kill the author of life as well (Luke 11:47–48). On the topic of killing, Jesus adjudges the Pharisees along with the other religious leaders to be pastoral imposters and false shepherds (in the spiritually destructive and ultimately deadly sense), who came "only to steal and kill and destroy" the sheep of God. By contrast, the Lord came as the true, Good Shepherd who gives the sheep life "to the full" (John 10:10).

Jesus tells Israel's religious leaders that they are in danger of missing out on the kingdom of God and heaven altogether (see Matthew 21:28-31; Luke 13:30). As long as a swagger-infused worship continues to pump out of the hearts and dribble off the lips of insincere members of Israel's entrusted religious establishment, the possibility of their names being found in the "Lamb's book of life" and a place reserved for them around the banquet table at the marriage feast of the Lamb remains in dire doubt.

For a so-called elite group of people—who likely presume they'll be the *first* to enter God's kingdom—to be told that they could actually be the *last* to go in—if at all—would be an ultra-offensive slap in their prideful faces. Regardless, Jesus Christ, as the enthroned and righteous judge of all souls, is the only one in perfect position to make such pronouncements (see 2 Corinthians 5:10; 2 Timothy 4:1).

I can vividly recall how one of my seminary professors cautioned his class to shy away from making the types of judgments that pronounce with all certainty a given person's eternal destiny. "We're going to be surprised by who we see in heaven, just as we're going to be surprised by who didn't make it," the professor commented.

It was a press-the-reset-button moment for my developing theology as a young pastor in training. The underlying point my professor was making is that only God can truly distinguish those who belong to Him from those who do not, and some people who we think may not belong to Him *could* in fact already have their kingdom membership sewn up. Tim Keller comments, "Today's outspoken believer may be tomorrow's apostate, and today's outspoken unbeliever may be tomorrow's convert.

We must not make settled, final decisions about anyone's spiritual state or fate."[18]

There are individuals who appear as though they've passed the Bible's test for salvation with flying spiritual colours but may actually be flunking. Conversely, people who appear to be far from believing in Jesus may be several spiritual miles *ahead* of where we think they are on the road *to* salvation (e.g. the tax collectors and sinners that the Pharisees often disparaged).

The enigmatic members of the religious sect could attend all the earthly banquets their hearts desired; one thing the Pharisees couldn't do, as echoed by the portents of Jesus, was claim reservations to the marriage feast of the Lamb in heaven when the bride of Christ (His church) is joined to Him (her groom). By their refusal (at least the majority of them) to endorse any opinion attesting to Jesus's divinity and their choice instead to pester Him for proof of such claims, scores of leaders among Israel's religious representative sects were cruising to die in their sin (John 8:21). The Pharisees were especially caught up with being right about who was fit to be in the presence of God and who wasn't; consequently, they dismissed Jesus's multiple warnings that *they* were the ones who were on an eternally lethal collision course with the judgment of God.

REFLECTIVE QUESTIONS

1. What expectations of the Messiah did Israel have that made it difficult for the people to believe in Jesus as their promised deliverer (Messiah), to the point where they had Him executed?
2. What problems did the Pharisees have with Jesus's teachings and actions?
3. Taking into consideration the content of this chapter, as well as the evidence in the Gospels, how would you explain why Jesus was so scathing in His critique of the Pharisees?
4. What does the Bible and Jesus specifically teach about the accountability of leaders and teachers of God's people? Why should such positions not be entered into lightly?
5. In your estimation, how were the Pharisees perceived and treated by those within Israel? Provide specific evidence from the Gospels.

---

[18] Timothy Keller, *The Reason for God: Belief in an Age of Skepticism* (New York: Riverhead Books, 2008), 83.

6. How did Jesus's righteous character and ministry differ from that of Israel's religious leaders?
7. In what ways might the Gospels' portrayal of the Pharisees relate to how some unbelievers and "unchurched" people today perceive clergy and organized religion?
8. How much of a shock do you think it would have been for both the common people and the outcasts of Jesus's day to hear the Lord's warnings concerning the possible eternal destinies of Israel's celebrated religious leaders (the Pharisees and others)?
9. How should Christians view God's judgment of *them* in eternity? Provide biblical passages to support your answer.

CHAPTER SIX

A SQUANDERED INVITATION

We live in a time of increasing self-centredness and skepticism. Consequently, people are said to be less likely to commit to anything. We're not as trusting or believing about anything anymore. In today's social economy, one's "rights" seem more valued than one's responsibility and one's prerogative more worthy than one's promise. We are far less confident of our leaders than we used to be, and we're even more fearful of them curtailing our freedoms. In some sense, Israel's treatment of Jesus Christ as He ministered among the nation mirrors the world's current attitudinal credo: "Trust nothing and no one."

Israel was expecting a prophet like one of Moses's ilk who'd possess the very words of God in their mouth (Deuteronomy 18:18). With this promise came certain messianic expectations. God indeed sent various spokesmen and women to His people throughout the generations, one replacing the other, all the way up to the point when God's promise of a coming prophet would be uniquely fulfilled in His Son, Jesus Christ.

God's people nursed a "we shall see" mentality when it came to committing to Jesus of Nazareth. Although a healthy number believed He was the one who was to come, far more weren't quite as eager to put their nation's hope in His kingdom, opting instead to treat Him as if He were merely the latest messianic flavour of the month and, of course, much worse.

God desired that the ancient Hebrew people be the archetypical nation whose king and ruler was their God (a theocracy). But Israel balked at the notion that Yahweh should be their national leader, that God Himself was the wisest option for leading an untrustworthy pack of wayward people like themselves! The Israelites wanted to be like the surrounding nations and asked God to install a human king over them. He gave them what they wished for.

The first monarch of Israel (Saul) didn't work out so hot, and neither would many of the other throne-sitters who'd follow through the centuries. Sadly, the sum of the Old Testament displays how often God's chosen people attempted to wrest the spiritual reins of their nation from His hands only to chart their own folly-filled course.

When their long-anticipated redeemer appeared out of Galilee in the person of Jesus Christ, God was essentially presenting His weary people of Israel with a Saviour-sized coda.

It's as if He was saying to them, *Time out! Let's go back to My redemptive plan for you and go over once again the requirement for your salvation and what righteous living looks like. While I'm at it, let Me introduce you to the only one who can save you and make you righteous before Me. Ladies and gentlemen of Israel, and all members of the human race, meet My people's Messiah and the Saviour of the world ... My Son, Jesus!*

The advent of Jesus signalled not a change in key concerning God's redemptive will for Israel but rather an orchestrated crescendo amidst it! Through His incarnated Son, God purposed to redefine His covenant people's expectations regarding the spiritual restoration of their nation. In that light, the entirety of the Gospels represents an ongoing conversation God was having with the Jewish people. Consequently, Israel needed to do a rethink concerning Jesus of Nazareth. They needed to see the Son of God in the perfect light of who *He* was (and is and forever will be); only then could the chosen people begin to see themselves for who *they* were: in need of the saving power of Christ—the one they were treating and aiming to drop like a forgettable date.

ISRAEL'S OPPORTUNITIES TO RESPOND TO JESUS

The Gospels record a time when people had the unthinkable privilege of experiencing God in Christ up close and personal—close enough to feel His breath on their faces. The incarnated Jesus lived for roughly thirty-three years in His human body. The last three-plus years of our Lord's earthly life were spent around a rabble of people whose fascination with Him left little doubt as to the peculiar and unique efflux of His divinity. When the Saviour sent His disciples out to various villages in order to prep the people for His imminent visitation, He invariably supplied them with banquet invitations. The deadly price He'd pay for the sinners' admission into the marriage feast of the Lamb would far outweigh what it would ever cost them in faith to reserve their place *at* the event!

A great future banquet in the kingdom of God was a much-anticipated event in Israel. By virtue of their status of being God's chosen and treasured people, the advantaged nation was naturally invited to share in the heavenly festivities. The people of Israel had a leg-up on getting into the banquet—at least it was *supposed* to work out that way. However, as was often the case with its ancestors, the Israel of Jesus's day continued to exhibit characteristics of a spiritually rogue nation. Their obedience to God had unravelled to the point where they let the banquet invitation that was their birthright slip through their stubborn and foolish fingers.

Israel's invitation to the glorious messianic feast and their inheritance of the kingdom were based on God's covenant with them, reissued through His Son. The second person of the Trinity went out of His way (left heaven) and willingly put Himself in harm's way to make this a reality. Yet the ungrateful and disbelieving hands of an indifferent Israel held those invitations loosely. They greeted the Saviour with a rousing response of non-commitment, confusion, chaos, and ultimately crucifixion. God "with skin on" personally extended an invite to His heavenly feast to the chosen people and paid the price with His life.

It didn't help that the nation's religious leaders worked together to impede Israel's hearing and responding to the hard knocks of God's conviction on their hearts (Matthew 23:13–14). Consequently, those within Israel who decided to "take a flyer" on Jesus eventually ended up trashing their obviously paper-thin interest in Him.

Just as there are people in our spheres of influence who receive our sharing about Christ with a sizable grain of skepticism, there were people in Jesus's day that refused to go as far as accepting Him as Israel's long-expected and promised redeemer. Israel had plenty of opportunity to turn towards the Lord. Jesus came imploring His fellow Jews to believe that *in Him* the door to the kingdom of heaven was open like it never had been before, and that participation in its future banquet was a mere faith-response away.

SPURNED RSVPS

Jesus began His parable of the great banquet with the following statements: "A certain man was preparing a great banquet and invited many guests. At the time of the banquet he sent his servant to tell those who had been invited, 'Come, for everything is now ready'" (Luke 14:16–17).

It was Jewish custom to issue an initial invite to guests of a banquet that would be followed by a subsequent notice of the event's imminent readiness. The parable, then, assumes the social custom of an invitation in advance followed by an invitation at the time of the meal to those who had accepted the first invitation.[19] A rabbinic commentary on Lamentations 4:2 states that none of the men of Jerusalem "would attend a banquet unless he was invited twice" (*Lam. R. 4:2*). (In the ancient world, banquets and other elaborate events took a great deal of time to prepare.) It would seem from Jesus's words, then, that the "many" whom the master had initially invited to his banquet had already notified the servant of their intentions to attend.

However, at some point between their acceptance of the invitation to the banquet and the host's subsequent notice that everything was finally ready for the event to begin, the enthusiasm of those who'd previously RSVP'd plummeted. When it came time for the "many" (likely referring to the people of Israel) to put their commitment where their prior intentions were, the reasons for not going that they gave the servant to relay to his master came across like a peal of apathy.

The response of the invitees in the parable mirrors Israel's response to Jesus of Nazareth. Multitudes of His fellow Jewish people initially rushed to the Lord like a current sweeping through and dividing the land. In a

[19] Craddock, *Luke*, 178.

frenzied demonstration of fanfare, they came on strong to Jesus, only to blow Him off later with surprising ease. Eventually His fellow Jews would issue their Messiah a fistful of contempt as a send-off to His execution. In the fresh wake of His death on the cross, before the reality of an empty tomb began to set in to steal their satisfaction, the enemies of Christ no doubt enjoyed what they thought was their victory lap around Jerusalem.

God had fulfilled His promise to send His covenant people of Israel a deliverer. The spectacular emergence of Jesus of Nazareth marked the fulfillment of centuries upon centuries of Jewish hopes and longings for a national redeemer. Granted, Jesus was the furthest thing from an iron-like conqueror waving a menacing sword and stirring up an army of supporters. Neither did our Lord appear as some celestial-like avatar wielding militant angels at His disposal that would surely melt the hubris of Rome like runny wax. Instead, God's people got a gentle Saviour wrapped in the skin of a suffering servant, a redeemer who came wielding nothing but invitations to the kingdom He brought with Him from heaven.

The Gospel accounts of Jesus's parables of the wedding feast and the great banquet point to a one-way road stretching from our current age into eternity to a time when the God whom we presently cannot look at and live to tell about it will be so incredibly present to us that we'll be able to ask Him to "pass the butter," as it were, at His banquet table! In a shocking turn of events that stung heaven and shook the world (literally), an abundantly blessed and uniquely privileged Israel excused themselves from the long-promised heavenly banquet that was meant to be their homecoming.

Regardless, in Jesus, every single person on earth has the hope of redemption. Paul rightly exclaimed that "all the promises of God find their Yes in him" (2 Corinthians 1:20, ESV). As we'll see, the empty seats around the heavenly banquet table at the marriage feast of the Lamb that were reserved for God's chosen people would come to be occupied by people who'd humbly RSVP in order to dine with Jesus for eternity.

REFLECTIVE QUESTIONS

1. Have you ever accepted an invitation to attend a party or event and then changed your mind? What were the reasons you had for subsequently declining?

2. Taking an oath was a part of Israel's societal practices and in certain cases even commanded in the Law. For Jesus, all words are binding. He simply taught us to keep our word. Is letting your "yes" be "yes" and "no" be "no" difficult for you to honour (Matthew 5:33–37; see also James 5:12)?
3. Have you ever wondered what the marriage feast of the Lamb will be like? See Matthew 22:2–14.
4. How often do you contemplate the fact that as a Christian you'll be able to experience Jesus like never before when you get into eternity? How does this impact your faith on *this* side of eternity?
5. Do you believe that the Holy Spirit's knock on the heart of those who repeatedly refuse Christ grows fainter with every passing attempt to convict them? Provide scriptural evidence for your answer.
6. Many people say they are "religious" or "spiritual" but live lives that show no evidence of possessing a saving faith. What sort of vices and interests are people filling their lives with today that distract and deceive them and cause them to grow indifferent to the Bible's claims concerning Jesus?
7. How does this statement impact you: "In Jesus every single person on the earth has the hope of redemption"?

CHAPTER SEVEN

EXCUSES— DECLINING AN INVITATION TO THE BANQUET

"But they all alike began to make excuses." (Luke 14:18)

I had a pretty good racket going when I was in elementary school. I made a habit of talking my mother into writing a note to excuse me from everything from taking gym to participating in classroom phonics to going to the school dentist. About the only excuse I didn't have my mother make for me was that "the dog ate my homework" (we had cats). You name the school function, I could persuade my dear mom to get me out of it.

People make excuses for just about everything. "I can't because ..." is an often used phrase. At one time or another we are all guilty of using excuses to get out of doing something, helping someone, or going somewhere. Sadly, excuses can become commonplace even in the life of well-intentioned Christians.

God's people make excuses to justify why they can't serve in at least one church ministry and why they don't pray as often as they should, why they can't attend church services on a consistent basis, and why they have time for everything but reading the Bible. There are legitimate reasons for the things we do or can't or won't do in life, and then there are simply excuses!

A HISTORY OF EXCUSES

When you read the parable of the great banquet it's hard not to catch a whiff of a practice that is, in fact, as old as the Garden of Eden: excuse making. The account in Genesis features excuse making. We could call it a "grassroots" movement! Remember Adam's riposte when the Lord asked him and Eve why they were camouflaging themselves in the bushes as He called out to them? Adam and Eve were no doubt hoping to stay hidden within the shadows of guilt. But when God's push came to Adam's shove, the world's first husband ended up blaming his wife for leading him into sin. Nice. Little did Adam realize that his convenient silence when the Mrs. was contemplating eating the forbidden fruit implicated him along with her!

Eve, of course, would play the blame game as well. She pointed a desperate accusatory finger at the cunning reptile that slithered into her presence (and thoughts), tempting her to second-guess the clear command of God (see Genesis 3:13). The devil may have interfered in the first marriage, but the decision to disregard the directive of God was all Adam and Eve's! In the wake of their freshly fallen spiritual natures and ensuing sin, all they could offer their Creator were ultra-flimsy excuses for not obeying Him. The art of excuse making would go on to become standard spiritual practice for some of the people of Israel.

In the parable of the great banquet we see a reflection of this cavalier approach to Yahweh. The long-anticipated eschatological banquet was the chosen people's to attend. All they needed to do was take the invitation from God's Son and confirm their place at His table. Instead, many sent their regrets wrapped in creatively constructed excuses.

THE THREE EXCUSES

Each person the master's servant invites in the parable of the great banquet gives him a line as to why they can't make the event. We can view the three excuses as paralleling Israel's standoffish demeanour towards the person and ministry of Jesus Christ.

The first invitee mentioned responds to the servant (and I paraphrase), "You know what? I just bought myself a field, and I'm dying to check it out for the first time. You dig? Ciao!" The master's servant proceeds to the second invitee, announcing that his master's banquet is all ready. However, the servant gets the same response, albeit with a few words changed here and there: "I just bought some oxen, you see, and I haven't even tried them out yet. Sorry about the banquet. No can do!" To say that both responses are greatly lacking in genuineness would be an understatement. How many people do you know who would purchase property or any other significant item without first assessing its value and usefulness?

Fresh off two nos and possibly headed for a third turndown, the servant goes to yet another person who had previously accepted an invite to his master's banquet. The third invitee's reason for declining the invitation, though an excuse all the same, at least sounds reasonable enough—something to the effect of "Sorry, but the banquet's no longer on my radar. I just got hitched, and I feel a honeymoon coming on. You know what I mean?"

The three individuals Jesus cites in the parable who initially accept an invitation to the banquet only to later decline each gives off their own fragrance of excuse making.

Notably, not all biblical commentators interpret the three regrets as being analogous to the Jews' refusal of Jesus. Richard L. Rohrbaugh argues that the three reasons given for abstaining from participation in the banquet are indicative of "elite Christians within Luke's own community refusing table fellowship with the poor."[20] R. Kent Hughes argues that the three regrets "reveals humankind's universal rejection of the kingdom … This text is talking about us and our preferences … The hardest people to reach are those who … bow toward God's Word but are unwilling to come to the feast."[21]

Still other scholars accept the three individuals as being symbolic of Israel's repeated attempts at keeping Jesus comfortably at bay and their failure to embrace Him as their Messiah. It makes for a sad spiritual commentary on the religious climate of a nation and people who should've been able to spot God's promised redeemer in the person and ministry of Jesus of Nazareth.

---

[20] Richard L. Rohrbaugh, "The Pre-Industrial City in Luke-Acts: Urban Social Relations," in *The Social World of Luke-Acts: Models for Interpretation*, ed. Jerome H. Neyrey (Peabody: Hendrickson, 1991), 125–149, 143.

[21] R. Kent Hughes, *Luke: That You May Know the Truth*, Preaching the Word (Wheaton: Crossway Books, 2015), 551–52.

ANCIENT ISRAEL: AN EXCUSE-LADEN NATION

The three individuals Jesus mentions in the parable of the great banquet who expressed their regrets to the servant for not being able to attend his master's event find a parallel in Israel's reputation for demonstrating indifference towards the goodness of Yahweh. God's short-sighted people were often ultra-relaxed with their end of the covenant that God made with them, without thinking of the long-term consequences for being so. No amount of reasons or excuses could validate the Israelites' pattern of taking for granted their standing with God.

We crack open the Old Testament and get reacquainted with Israel's ill-conceived reasons for not obeying the God of their redemption. Complaints and cop-outs demonstrated their meagre commitment to and thankfulness for their God.

Allow me to jog your memory with the use of a little paraphrasing: We know we don't have any other food, but we don't care for those crispy wafers you keep dropping on us, Lord … Moses looked like he couldn't get with the program so we ditched him! … We were just comparing life in this horrible desert with living in Egypt under Pharaoh, that's all … We thought a little idol worship here and there wouldn't harm anyone … We don't care how wonderful the Promised Land may be; we have this aversion to giants, you see?

If it wasn't their murmurings of dissatisfaction and moans of ungratefulness in the wilderness of Sinai, it was the Israelites' short memory where Yahweh's parting of the Red Sea was concerned. If their repeated failures to obey their God's commands and regulations weren't foolish enough, their manufacturing of a golden calf to worship took the irreverent cake.

Speaking through the prophet Jeremiah hundreds of years later, God called His perpetually delinquent people to His throne's carpet.

> "What fault did your ancestors find in me, that they strayed so far from me? They followed worthless idols and became worthless themselves. They did not ask, 'Where is the LORD, who brought us up out of Egypt and led us through the barren wilderness, through a land of deserts and ravines, a land of drought and utter darkness, a land where no one travels and no one lives?' I brought you into a fertile land to eat its fruit and rich produce. But you

came and defiled my land and made my inheritance detestable." (Jeremiah 2:5–7)

We know this from reading the Old Testament: Israel and a brigade of excuses went hand in hand! Despite their repeated infidelities as a nation, Yahweh had kept the covenant He made with their forefathers to redeem them from slavery. He plucked an obscure people from no man's land and subsequently placed them in the Promised Land. He took them from a ragtag nomadic existence under Abraham and turned them into a blessed and feared nation under the likes of Moses and Joshua.

However, by the time of Jesus, Israel's rap sheet of godless rebellion and excuse making was as long as it was legendary. Many of God's people seemed to possess genes that made it quite easy for them to rebuff whatever sounded like a prophetic voice calling them to heel to truth and turn from their national apostasy—*even if that voice came from God, born and bred among them!* The Lord's pursuit of His fellow Jewish people's hearts coupled with His pleas (even via the miraculous) for them to believe in Him—even as many in Israel kept looking the other way—underscore how spiritually desensitized the nation had become (see John 12:37).

The apostle Paul said it best when he reckoned that Israel's zeal for God was not based on "knowledge" (see Romans 10:2–4). As a Jew, the apostle was preaching what he'd once practised. Perhaps even the pioneering Christian missionary and preeminent New Testament theologian at one time utilized excuses to try to defuse any sparks the other-worldly actions and words of Jesus produced. In fact, Paul had made it his pharisaical obsession to pursue every proviso within the Jewish law to justify punishing those who *did* believe in the Lord's divinity.

As unimaginable it may seem from the perspective of Paul's spiritual and highly fruitful transformation following his conversion experience on the Damascus Road, a pre-converted Paul surely would've owned the same sentiments concerning the Saviour that made many a religious leader in Israel lose sleep. We can just hear a raging Saul: "This Jesus can't possibly be our Messiah! He's too un-Law like! He's too sinner-schmoozy! Too leper-loving! He's too criminal-cavorting and Gentile-genial to be a Jew, let alone our meal ticket to a restored kingdom of Israel!"

How ironic that Jesus indeed came as His people's ticket to a meal like none other, a banquet in heaven set for those whom the Lord reached out

His hands to all day long. But He found so few takers and more than a few excuse-makers! The nation repeatedly demonstrated spiritual blindness in the face of God's *visible* work of grace in their midst—right up to the time of the unveiling of their Messiah, Jesus.

In the culture of Jesus's day it was a grievous offence to the host of a banquet for an invitee to decline the second invitation, as if he were unworthy of the guest. In fact, guests were thought to be duty-bound to obey multiple invitations to an event such as a banquet.

The servant in the parable could already hear his master's fury-filled response to the revelation that those who had previously accepted an invitation to his banquet were now backing out one by one. Indeed, the master *did* take umbrage at hearing the servant's report. "The servant came back and reported this to his master. Then the owner of the house became angry and ordered his servant, 'Go out quickly into the streets and alleys of the town and bring in the poor, the crippled, the blind and the lame'" (Luke 14:21).

SILVER LININGS

The resourceful servant knew a side of his master that was big-hearted and soft. As a result, he had already begun to pound the dusty back roads of human hopelessness in search of dwellers on the threshold of dignity gone adrift. This is the *second* invitation Jesus speaks of in the parable of the great banquet.

When the servant found those who were impoverished and physically challenged they too were issued an invitation to his master's banquet—and not a hair of resistance could be found on these surely overjoyed folks! Never mind the sound of another mite tinkling in their begging cups out of someone's goodwill; this time their ship had come in, and it turned out to be a yacht!

Only God possesses the kind of gracious heart that extends invitations to as many banquet invitees as possible. The silver lining in this parable, then, is seen in the master's (God's) benevolence overcoming the initial invitees' subterfuge.

"The original guests have ruled themselves out ... Once again the expected guests are the Jews, waiting and waiting for the kingdom, only to find, when it arrived, that they had more pressing things to occupy them ... Clearly many Jews were part of Jesus' kingdom-movement from the beginning. But the majority of the nation, both in Palestine and in the scattered Jewish communities in the rest of the world, were not. Instead ... God's messengers had gone out into the roads and hedgerows of the world, getting all kinds of unexpected people to join in the party."[22]

Thus, underprivileged persons would be blessed on account of God's privileged people boycotting His Son and, consequently, the kingdom He'd brought with Him from heaven.

In Scripture, God's call to us is to drop *all* and follow Him. His invitation to us to accept and follow His Son, Jesus, is *the* most important request to tend to in our lives, no matter how seemingly inconvenient and ill-timed it may appear (see Matthew 8:18–22). Our best laid plans in life—as justifiable and profitable as they may seem to us—should never take precedence over God's more urgent and greater plan and will for our lives. "God's offer has priority not simply over our worst but also over our best agendas. Those who attend [the banquet] do so not because there was nothing else to do but because the banquet was the best among attractive alternatives."[23]

REFLECTIVE QUESTIONS

1. Would people describe you as a person who makes a lot of excuses? What is your honest opinion of yourself in relation to this topic?
2. It's been said that we're becoming an increasingly selfish society. This reality can influence God's people. What kinds of reasons do you hear fellow believers give for not being able to be more consistent in attending Sunday services and getting involved in the ministry of the church? (Be careful of being hypocritical!)
3. How do the three excuses given in the parable of the great banquet mirror our society's championing of self-centredness and indifference to spiritual things?
4. Do you see any parallels between the Israelites' rebellious treatment of Yahweh, and to a lesser degree Moses, and Israel's reaction to the person and ministry of Jesus Christ?

---

[22] Tom Wright, *Luke For Everyone* (Louisville: Westminster John Knox Press, 2004), 177–178.

[23] Craddock, *Luke*, 179.

5. Compare your experiences in encountering people who see themselves as being "religious" and people who exhibit clear apathy towards spiritual things.
6. Name some of the excuses unbelieving people use to avoid giving their lives to Christ and living under His Lordship.
7. Read Matthew 8:18–22. Discuss what you believe are the underlying points Jesus was making to those who wanted to follow Him.

CHAPTER

EIGHT

THE CONSEQUENCE OF REJECTING AN INVITATION TO THE BANQUET

"I tell you, not one of those men who were invited will get a taste of my banquet." (Luke 14:24)

Most Christians are familiar with the bumper-sticker-like phrase "No Jesus, No Peace; Know Jesus, Know Peace." It makes sense to the twenty-first century believer. The letter to the Romans teaches that in order for people to have "peace with God" they must possess faith in His Son, which justifies their standing and acceptance before Him (5:1). The work of salvation was completed by Jesus on Calvary's cross; now, the spiritually lost need only believe in Christ to be saved (Acts 16:31). Such preaching, however, was a major stumbling block to many in Israel, apparently even for some who had *already* put their faith in Jesus of Nazareth! The ministry of Moses—one of the most revered figures in Israel—ran deep within their nation's religious bloodstream.

In that light, it was undoubtedly difficult for the Jews to hear, let alone come to terms with, the fact that not only was Jesus greater than Moses, but His sacrifice alone was sufficient for their redemption because it rendered the requirements of the Law observed in full! Both Jews and

Gentiles, as one recognized people (believers), were being incorporated into the Body of Christ (the church) and were therefore *equally* covered under His blood for the forgiveness of their sins. Consequently, they were equally eligible for admission into the much-anticipated eschatological banquet in the last day.

In Acts 15, Luke introduces a group of distinguished Jewish men who had become followers of Jesus. Normally this would have been encouraging news within the leadership stratosphere of the young Christian church. However, these same individuals apparently couldn't quite bring themselves to the point of cutting the cord that kept them attached and enslaved to regulations within the Old Testament Law. These legalists, as they were known in the first century, had been teaching Gentiles in Antioch—who themselves were freshly converted to Christ—that their salvation would be null and void "unless [they were] circumcised, according to the custom taught by Moses" (Acts 15:1). A theological switcheroo of that magnitude would have registered as spiritually head-scratching to the new believers, who surely must have wondered what became of the "just come to Jesus" sermons they'd heard preached by the apostles!

Luke identified a contingent of Jewish believers who were present in Jerusalem as having belonged to the party of the Pharisees. Predictably, this faction endorsed what the individuals were teaching the Gentiles in Antioch. This brought on a doctrinal migraine among the church's apostolic circle. These emerging Jewish teachers were essentially promoting that in order for Gentile Christians to truly be saved by *faith* they were required to become converts to *Judaism* first. Talk about a totally inverted presentation of the gospel of Jesus Christ! Thankfully, these misguided teachers—who the New Testament labels as Judaizers—had their spiritual impairment rectified by the early church's pillars of spiritual authority in Jerusalem.

At a convened council in that city, the leading apostles affirmed that followers of Christ were not required to be Old-Testament-Law-abiding citizens in the sense of their eternal salvation depending on continued adherence to commandments in the Mosaic Law. The nascent church's leaders connected the dots of the Old Testament's prophecies concerning Israel's promised redeemer to Jesus Christ. Rightfully, then, the apostles taught that only Jesus *could* and *did* fulfill to perfection the righteous commands of the Law and that that accomplishment (*His* righteousness) was to be accredited to those whose faith abided in *Him* as the Saviour (see Acts 15:8–11; Romans 3:20–23, 5:19).

The apostles' bottom line to the Judaizers concerning Gentile conversion, therefore, was simple: no amount of obeyed commandments from the old order could possibly equal the all-sufficient ministry of Jesus to save sinners in the here and now—for the Jew as well as the Gentile (see Colossians 2:13–15; Hebrews 10:1–10).

For those Jews who put their hope for true redemption in Jesus's ministry, the apostles' message certainly got across. Such persons possessed an unalloyed adherence to the Saviour. For other Jews, however, there was no talking them down from their defiant view that Jesus of Nazareth was nothing more than another name and face put to still another inane "freedom" movement that predictably flopped. Incredibly, those for whom the door into God's kingdom (and His banquet table) was held wide open would fail to enter it.

The last line Luke recorded from Jesus's parable of the great banquet comes across as stunningly final. The Lord always knew how to *end* a story for desired effect. Upon hearing his servant's report that the privileged invitees to his banquet spurned his goodwill, the indignant master—aside from directing his servant to invite others—resolved, "I tell you, not one of those who were invited will get a taste of my banquet" (Luke 14:24).

Should we surmise from these words that the master was an unfair, ungracious, and unforgiving person? Hardly! The master opened his banquet up to virtually any and all persons, regardless of who they were or where they came from. By ending His parable on a hopeless, harsh note, Jesus calls those in His presence to chew on the gloomy implications of the parable's closing argument. The Lord issues a "hear Me right" portent in that the Jews' refusal to accept God's invitation to salvation in Him would result in not just the inclusion of the Gentiles into the heavenly kingdom but also their own *exclusion* from it (see Matthew 21:43).

That said, it is also important to note that the last line of the parable shouldn't be taken in the unalterable sense, as in no one from Israel will *ever* enter the kingdom of God. Rather, Jesus aims to stress the eternal consequences one faces (Jew or Gentile) for rejecting God's kingdom invitation in Him.

ENTERING THE KINGDOM OF GOD

In this parable Jesus conveyed that just because Israel was blessed with an invitation to enter into His eternal kingdom, it *didn't* mean the nation possessed an *automatic* claim to it or a free pass. The grace of God always demands a response of faith from its object of blessing. The Jews, as is the case with all other people and nations, must respond to God's gracious invitation by exhibiting a *saving* faith in His Son; it's the only response that will give the people of Israel cause to claim any inheritance in His kingdom.

It's not like God is enforcing a new rule for how His chosen people must enter the kingdom of heaven. Jesus Christ always has been *the* inheritance long-promised to Israel. Knowing that He was the very fulfillment of the festival He was attending, Jesus took the opportunity to openly proclaim, "Let anyone who is thirsty come to me and drink. Whoever believes in me, as Scripture has said, rivers of living water will flow from within them" (John 7:37–38).

When He came in the flesh proclaiming that the kingdom of God was at hand, Jesus Christ was putting Israel on notice. They would be held accountable for the fact that the Saviour had come directly to their nation's doorstep. The Lord couldn't have been more comprehensible in His pronouncement that He is the sole Way-maker, Truth-bearer, and Life-giver, bridging the eternal life-and-death divide that separates lowly sinners from a holy God (see John 14:6).

The author of Hebrews warned Jewish converts to Christianity who were teetering on the cliff of reverting back to Judaism (and thus committing apostasy) that just as the Israelites' physical, temporal rest in Canaan demanded faith in Yahweh's promise, so salvation rest can only be entered into by means of obedience to the Lord (see Hebrews 4:6–11). The believers' Sabbath rest is seen in the finished work of Christ on the cross and in their harmonious involvement in His salvation program.

The "Coles Notes" version of that warning is simply this: No Jesus equals no entrance into the kingdom of God and no share in the eschatological feast He'll host in the company of all He made righteous, an event that's inextricably lodged within the national expectations and religious beliefs of the Jewish people.

The Bible assures us of the one sure-fire way to secure our ultimate rest and eternal security in heaven. It's a passage that bears nothing but *good* news: "For God so loved the world that he gave his one and only Son, that whoever believes in him shall not perish but have eternal life" (John 3:16).

I've often thought that when Christians quote John 3:16 to the unsaved, they really ought to be quoting John 3:36 as well. In contrast to the first one, this one contains nothing but *bad* news: "But whoever rejects the Son will not see life, for God's wrath remains on them" (John 3:36).

So when people mulishly dismissed the redeemer God sent to take their sin away, they needed to know that such a decision stranded them on an overcrowded and spiritually destructive road (see Matthew 7:13). And those who were relying on their righteous deeds to get them into heaven needed to know that they were headed for a rather shocking eternal discovery and irreversible destiny (see Matthew 7:21–23; Ephesians 2:8–9). Such was the foolish thinking of some who kicked the Saviour's tires in hopes of validating their own righteousness.

A lot of people didn't mind catching the sensational waves Jesus's ministry was making. However, for some, when it came time for them to face facts about their own spiritual need and need of the Saviour, they wiped out (e.g. the rich young ruler in Mark 10:17–27). Miracles and exorcisms easily drew crowds and resulted in the amazement and approval of many. However, just because one walked along with Jesus and gawked at His supernatural powers didn't necessarily mean he or she was moving any closer to the Pearly Gates. The Lord wasn't calling people to pretend they were a part of His kingdom; He was calling those who were intrigued with Him to become the "real deal" in terms of being His disciples. A skin-deep lip-service brand of faith in Him would never cut it with the Son of God.

The saddest earthly road leading to hell isn't the one paved with good intentions; it's the one travelled with faulty expectations of eternity. We all know people who baselessly claim to have a natural right to enter into some blessed and peaceful afterlife. They believe they will attain such a destination irrespective of the fact that their lives fall short of revealing a saving faith in Jesus Christ (the standard for salvation in the Bible). Paul, in his letter to the Christians in Colossae, prayed that the believers in that city would be filled "with the knowledge of [God's] will ... live a life worthy of the Lord and please him in every way: bearing fruit in every good work, growing in the knowledge of God" (Colossians 1:9–10). For Paul, these manifestations of the Spirit's work were evidence of a truly redeemed life.

VINES—AND AN UNFRUITFUL ISRAEL

Using an agricultural image familiar to first century peasants, Jesus declared Himself to be the "true vine" whom His disciples needed to "remain in" if their lives were to exhibit spiritual fruitfulness and vitality (John 15:1–6; see also 1 John 2:6). In fact, the Lord cautioned those who followed Him that they'd have *no* spiritual fruit-bearing ability *apart* from their union and fellowship with Him.

Agriculture 101 says any branch detached from its mother-vine and thrown away can only yield two results: fruitlessness and, ultimately, lifelessness! Unfortunately, this basic lesson in agriculture finds a symbolic (and spiritual) parallel in the history of God's chosen people. Israel, in the Old Testament, is referred to as a vine in both negative *and* positive language. Yahweh purposed to bring Abraham and the people who would come from him (the Israelites) to a land He would show them; once they were there, He would plant, root, and grow them in the same sense as a fruitful vine, a vine that was meant to sprawl and spread from its holy home base in Canaan to the surrounding pagan regions as a testimony to the one true God.

Although the Bible ultimately expresses hope for the eventual replanting of this vine—Israel, there were intervals in the nation's life where for all the Lord's cultivating of His precious vine, Israel's insatiable appetite for reckless disobedience rendered them a vine fit for the fire pits of His wrath (see Psalm 80:8; Ezekiel 15, 17; Hosea 10:1).

The Lord planted Israel to be a true vine, intending them to bear fruit. The Old Testament prophets explain that bearing fruit requires living lives of faithful worship to God, and as Israel demonstrated faithful living, God would bring light to the world. Israel mostly failed to live as a true vine, but God sent Jesus as the ultimate true vine, succeeding where Israel failed.

The parable of the great banquet, if anything, underscores the eternal cost one pays for sidestepping His Son. Simply, a life lived without Christ will not only preclude you from truly experiencing the power of God on *this* side of eternity; it will inevitably prohibit you from enjoying the endless glory and peace of God *in eternity*.

Still, this was the option chosen by a deceived Israel. God was forming a new covenant (a fuller administration of His grace, sealed by the death of Jesus) between Him and those redeemed of the Lord (see Luke 22:20; Jeremiah 31:31–34). The *old* covenant, with its ball-and-chain-like yoke of commandments, had a best-before date (see Hebrews 10:1–10). This was something that numerous Jewish Christians (notably the Judaizers of Acts 15) had tremendous difficulty wrapping their new-found faith around. The Jews needed to get out from behind the apron of the Law long enough to be able to cling to the cross of Christ—the redeemer whom so many among His own people of Israel rejected so cavalierly.

REFLECTIVE QUESTIONS

1. Why did the Judaizers (legalists) seem to equate the ministry of Jesus with the likes of Moses and the Law in the transaction of Gentile salvation? Consider the events of Acts 15 and the content of Galatians 3.
2. How might a legalistic leaning or understanding of faith issues complicate how one communicates the gospel to the spiritually lost?
3. The early church, which was predominantly Jewish, faced enormous opposition from their own people of Israel. In what ways does this mirror the unfortunate reality of "friendly fire" that exists within the church?
4. Put yourself in the shoes of a first century Jewish person. You hear Jesus tell you that unless you believe in Him (irrespective of observing the Law) you will die in your sins, miss out on the heavenly kingdom entirely, and suffer eternally. In addition to this, you're told by Jesus that Gentiles—who generally do not observe the Law and are not understood to be people of the promise—will go in your stead. What kinds of thoughts, emotions, and attitudes might Jesus's words stir up within you that could influence how you act towards those who follow Him (the church)?
5. The apostle Paul writes in Colossians that those who will "share in the inheritance of [God's] holy people" should invariably exhibit—among other redemptive evidence—a life that demonstrates a "knowledge

of God" and "fruit in every good work" (1:10–14). Using your home church as the context, are you aware as to whether there is a process in place to ensure that people in the congregation are saved and growing spiritually?

6. Optional: Place a bowl of fresh grapes beside a few grapes cut from their vine a number of days before. Compare the difference in the quality of the grapes and discuss how it illustrates what Israel was meant to be spiritually and what was often the reality as a nation (weak, soft, and separated from the blessing of God).
7. Read John 15:1–10. How does Jesus's teaching in these verses parallel the vine imagery in regard to Israel and God's judgment of them?

CHAPTER

NINE

OUTCASTS RECEIVE BANQUET INVITATIONS

"Go out quickly into the streets and alleys of the town and bring in the poor, the crippled, the blind and the lame." (Luke 14:21)

Jesus is different. That's why He makes a difference. One of the ways in which His kingdom differs from popular thought is in appearance. Jesus dines with tax collectors and sinners and does things on the Sabbath He ought not to do according to the prevailing interpretations of the Law and the traditions of the elders. It seems like the Saviour enjoys a little boat-rocking!

Our Lord takes on all comers and opens the gates to heaven wide enough to take in typically overlooked people who suffer the social stigma of being deemed *outcasts.* Individuals in the vicinity of Israel left out and left to wander emotionally, physically, and spiritually become eligible for the acquisition of dignity, mercy, and a banquet invitation!

People deemed outcasts in our Lord's time often flee *toward* Jesus, not away from Him. The worse a person feels about himself or herself, the more likely that he or she sees Jesus as a refuge and His kingdom a safe place. Mary Magdalene (or Mary of Magdala) is certainly one of those people.

THE BENEVOLENT MINISTRY OF JESUS

Mary is a woman familiar with grief. She knows what it feels like to be classified as a social orphan—an "undesirable"—in her culture. Before meeting Jesus, Mary suffered from demonic possession—a condition that surely would've been visible to many of her peers. She would have known what it was like to be avoided, shunned, and openly talked about maliciously.

It is especially controversial for the Lord to befriend someone like Mary. By choosing to hang out with the morally and ethically loose of His day, Jesus invites a plethora of shots at His reputation and qualifications as a perceived teacher of teachers. Predictably, the Pharisees and other religious leaders attack His friendship with her and others within the same troubled and ostracized camp. Yet it appears as though the Son of God prefers to mingle with the riff-raff than to "put on the Ritz," so to speak. Mary and others like her know that Jesus cares more about people in *need* of Him than about what ignorant people *think* of Him, that He cares more about the plight of undesirables than about the accusatory press and negative spin that always threaten to wrap around Him as a result of His association with such people. No wonder Mary remains alone at Jesus's empty tomb while the disciples Peter and John are nowhere to be found!

She is devoted to the Lord for the unconditional love He shows her. Jesus exorcized seven demons from Mary and by doing so restored her dignity. The compassion of God swallows up the grief in her life. Mary learns that in polar opposition to her prevailing culture's distaste for her kind, God *welcomes* the socially undesirable and discarded into His midst. Mary and many other needy outcasts like her learn that, through His sacrificially benevolent Son, God had gone to unfathomable lengths in order to invite such people to taste of His kingdom's bountiful fare of grace.

The Pharisees encouraged sharp and tight boundaries for society that excluded the very "outcasts" that are invited to the banquet. The "crippled, the blind and the lame" sought by the master's servant (Luke 14:21) are symbolic of God's summoning of a particular group of people whom many of Israel's leaders (from the perspective of a strict interpretation of Leviticus 21) believed were not in a naturally blessed position in life and, consequently, were unfit to worship at the temple. Such "defected" misfits and unfits in Jewish society were thought by some, especially those within the Qumran community, to be disqualified from the messianic banquet.[24] (Note: these are precisely the types of socially marooned people Jesus encourages the host Pharisee to invite to his feasts in Luke 14:13.)

SOCIAL MISFITS AND UNFITS ARE COMING TO THE GREAT BANQUET

According to Luke, Jesus's vision of a restored community of Israel differs from the usual patterns. Robert Tannehill comments, "The kingdom over which Jesus wants to rule must stretch to include people excluded by the holy people … Those marginalized by poverty, gender, and purity rules must be included. Jesus brings sinners and tax collectors into his fellowship. This is part of the restoration of Israel to wholeness."[25] Many of the undesirables among Jesus's contemporaries enter the banquet hall along with those from the highways "to become reconstituted Israel, the refashioned people of God."[26] The kingdom of God, then, "will not be a continuation of the present but a reversal of its exclusionary and discriminatory social codes."[27]

Jesus comes to redeem sinners and give them a foretaste of what the hymn writer Fanny Crosby described as "glory divine"—an earthly peek at heavenly realities, where the transformed *and* perfected version of person and soul awaits them. Just think of all the optometrists, pharmaceutical companies, psychologists, and counsellors—not to mention all the manufacturers of walkers and canes—the Lord would put out of business if He walked the earth today!

Jesus also stirs up hope for a liberated and revitalized Israel amid the dispiriting presence of the Roman Empire within the nation. What does Jesus *not* do to balance the scales of social injustice and get His own people to dream again?

In and through Jesus, Israel's God was brandishing a grace so magnetic it got every manner of undesirables racing and dropping at His feet, a

---

[24] Evans, *Luke*, 225.

[25] Robert C. Tannehill, *The Shape of Luke's Story: Essays on Luke–Acts* (Eugene: Cascade Books, 2005).

[26] Joseph Fitzmeyer, *The Gospel According to Luke X–XXIV,* Anchor Bible Commentary (New York: Doubleday, 1985), 1054.

[27] Gail R. O'Day, *Luke, John*, The New Interpreter's Bible, vol. IX, ed. Leander Keck (Nashville: Abingdon Press, 1995), 290.

repeated occurrence that motivated Jesus's detractors to burn much midnight oil in their attempts to put a stop to such spectacles. The Saviour's healing on the Sabbath and His touching of filthy undesirables was bad enough; acting like He could pardon sinners was way beyond intolerable to the religious bosses of Israel.

Over and against the prevailing prejudices towards the socially misfit and unfit in His day, Jesus pronounced the likes of the demon-possessed, the prostitute, and every other manner of so-called "unclean" persons eligible for entrance into heaven, the qualifier being that anyone who realized that they were spiritually "sick" needed to come to the Lord in contrition of heart. The Great Physician willed to heal and redeem the spiritually lost and repentant for the glory of God.

However, even though salvation is free, the grace of God is *not* inexpensive. One can freely come to Jesus as they are (in a spiritually fallen state), but it is never okay to stay as they are. As He so often did, Jesus commanded those He willed to save to sin no more (John 8:11).

Philip Yancey in *Vanishing Grace* writes, "In his ministry Jesus gave vivid proof that no one need fall below the reach of God's grace, not a prostitute, thief, murderer, or traitor. Indeed, Peter the traitor and Paul the human rights abuser, both now forgiven and transformed, proceeded to lead the way in spreading that gospel of grace."[28]

SPIRITUAL ARROGANCE VERSUS HUMILITY

At the heart of Israel's disdain for and treatment of the unclean and untouchable among them was their collective failure to recognize the presence, work, and kingdom intents of God manifested in His heaven-sent Son, Jesus of Nazareth. Many among Israel should have been able to pick up on the heart of their nation's God in the actions of Christ. Instead, they grossly miscalculated God's mercy and capacity to love even the perceived worst of sinners without divine "strings" attached. It didn't help matters that the Jews were also overlooking the gravity of their *own* spiritual uncleanness and neediness before the Lord. The religiously self-congratulating element among the Pharisees reckoned themselves fit and healthy and therefore in no need of seeing the doctor (Jesus) (see Matthew 9:12–13)!

[28] Philip Yancey, *Vanishing Grace: What Ever Happened to the Good News?* (Grand Rapids: Zondervan, 2014), 229.

The Lord always had a word for occasions when those "who were confident of their own righteousness and looked down on everyone else" exposed their folly in His presence (Luke 18:9). In the parable of the Pharisee and the tax collector, which may have been about an actual transaction Jesus witnessed, the Lord mentioned a certain publican (tax collector) who stood far off from God at the temple as he prayed in connection with the morning and evening Jewish sacrifices. As he prayed the publican beat his chest out of a sincere regret for his sin, while a cocky Pharisee standing close by proceeded to recount and even praise his own righteous acts before God (which were now compromised). If that weren't foolhardy enough, the audacious Pharisee began to deride others who failed to live up to his bloated standard of righteousness (like the contrite publican in his company) (see Luke 18:9–14).

Jesus teaches that prideful attitudes such as the one the Pharisee at the temple possessed offend the heart of God. The verdict the Lord renders concerning the two worshippers in His parable favours the publican. Jesus notes that out of the two, the publican is actually the one in the position of being blessed, "justified" by virtue of his self-incriminating evaluation and penitent state of heart in the presence of God.

Those within Israel who, like the humbled publican in Jesus's parable, were discarded and disparaged by their fellow countrymen yet accepted their spiritual brokenness before God would be welcomed into His kingdom's banquet hall and granted the prerogative of sitting at the table with God Himself! Humanly speaking, the world's rejects and refuse become heaven's reclamation projects on account of the "kindness" of God, who calls everyone to repentance (see Romans 2:4). This is the heartbeat of Almighty God for all needy sinners—for the Pharisee, the prostitute, and the publican alike—whom He wills should not "perish" eternally but come to a soul-saving knowledge of Jesus Christ (2 Peter 3:9).

Israel's iconic King David, while pursuing God's heart, realized that He is a God of mercy, a God who is loving towards and concerned for the welfare of all people, even the most depraved of sinners. David wrote, "Praise the LORD, O my soul, and forget not all his benefits—who forgives all your sins and heals all your diseases, who redeems your life from the pit and crowns you with love and compassion … the LORD works righteousness and justice for all the oppressed" (Psalm 103:2–4, 6).

By disqualifying themselves from participating in the blessings of the heavenly kingdom at the end of days, the unbelieving Jews unwittingly made room for others to go in their stead. Jesus's identification with and affinity for the socially stricken, the sick, and the stranger; for the forgotten, the forsaken, and the foreigner; for the outcast, the oppressed, and the overlooked; and for the least, the last, and the lonely suggest that the kingdom of God and His banquet table is meant for such people—as well as for those with more obvious and impressive religious and spiritual qualifications.

David keenly noted, "How priceless is your unfailing love, O God! People take refuge in the shadow of your wings. They feast on the abundance of your house; you give them drink from your river of delights" (Psalm 36:7–8). The king's life often imitated his faith in a merciful and charitable God. A prime example of this was when David extended kindness to Jonathan's physically challenged son Mephibosheth and his family by restoring their land and allowing them to eat at his table (2 Samuel 9:9–10). The benevolence David exhibited towards Mephibosheth was a foreshadow of the mercy God would demonstrate through His Son Jesus to all who are crippled spiritually by sin and who are invited to partake of His heavenly banquet!

The apostle Paul counselled the egotistical and carnal church in Corinth that pedigree, skill, and so-called wisdom are not what gets one into the kingdom of heaven. "God chose the lowly things of this world and the despised things—and the things that are not—to nullify the things that are, so that no one may boast before him" (1 Corinthians 1:28–29).

N. T. Wright punctuates this theme of God choosing to pursue those who are socially overlooked and undervalued with the instruction that Christians "must work out in their own churches and families what it would mean to celebrate God's kingdom so that people at the bottom of the pile, at the end of the line, would find it to be good news."[29]

Everyone qualifies for access to God. The parable of the great banquet confirms that God is not impressed when someone is on the higher planes of society, and neither is He depressed when someone is on the lower. Because into these social realities strode Jesus, the great Equalizer!

---

[29] Wright, *Luke for Everyone*, 179.

THE RHYTHM OF GOD'S COMPASSION AND THE MINISTRY OF JESUS'S CHURCH

The lines of Emma Lazarus's 1883 sonnet "The New Colossus" are inscribed on a bronze plaque located in the pedestal of the Statue of Liberty in New York. A portion of the sonnet states, "Keep, ancient lands, your storied pomp! … Give me your tired, your poor, your huddled masses yearning to breathe free, the wretched refuse of your teeming shore. Send these, the homeless, tempest-tost to me, I lift my lamp beside the golden door!"

At the time of this writing, the migrant crisis in the Middle East and Europe, predominantly, continues to wash up on the borders of numerous countries, a reality that renders Lazarus's forgotten (though no less relevant) sonnet a convicting commentary on the need for the most blessed and well-positioned of nations and people to remain charitable towards the plight of the displaced and destitute on their doorsteps.

There's an unparalleled opportunity for Christians worldwide to become a refugee's best friend, to love their neighbour by showcasing the unmatchable love of the gospel, a gospel that proclaims good news to the poor, freedom for those imprisoned (even within refugee camps), and new life for those fleeing from oppression, who are yearning to breathe free.

I often wonder whether the church today has lost its spiritual aptness for communicating the compassion Jesus possessed for the needy and ignoble, without any traces of spiritual pride, legalism, and judgment mixed in. Consequently, I wonder whether the down-and-outers and unfortunates that flocked to Jesus and found refuge in Him would feel as welcome among His followers today.

Our churches likely appear too pretty for some of the so-called undesirables within our communities and cities to feel comfortable in. This is why the ministry of Mother Teresa became a modern microcosm of the church of Jesus Christ *being* the church of Jesus Christ. How many poor, disease-ridden, and dying people strewn throughout the forsaken alleys of Calcutta did the revered Roman Catholic nun touch and rehumanize, as if she were doing it to the Lord Himself (see Matthew 25:34–40)?

The late Charles Colson's incarceration after he was found guilty for his part in the Watergate scandal changed the spiritual trajectory of his life—and then some! Colson would go from the White House to the courthouse to the "big house." As the founder of Prison Fellowship ministries, the former aide to President Nixon went from being an entitled politician to a compassionate minister of the Gospel to forgotten and despised prison inmates.

In his book *The Colson Way: Loving Your Neighbor and Living with Faith in a Hostile World,* Owen Strachan notes, "Colson had gone into jails, venturing boldly into places many Christians wanted to pretend did not exist … Colson's sense of compassion was awakened in prison. Being unable to aid others during his sentence left him with a lifelong thirst to help the needy. It was during the period in which he lost his own dignity that his desire to promote the dignity of others roared to life."[30]

The rhythm of compassion beating through Emma Lazarus's sonnet, which clearly pulsated through Charles Colson's ministry to prison inmates—and which is to be the standard for Jesus's church—is reflected as well in the charitable actions of the servant in the parable of the great banquet. People who were often treated and regarded as being subhuman in their first century society were approached by the servant and blessed with invitations to his master's banquet.

REFLECTIVE QUESTIONS

1. Are there any individuals in your church's worship services whom culture may deem as being "undesirables" (e.g. street people, the mentally challenged or mentally ill, or rougher or edgier looking people)?
2. How often do you associate with and even invite to your home those whom our culture ostracizes?
3. Taking into consideration passages in the Gospels accounting for Jesus's friendship with Mary Magdalene, what kinds of cultural taboos might Jesus have overridden by associating with her?
4. In what sorts of ways did the values of the kingdom Jesus inaugurated differ from the expectations of Israel's leaders—in particular, the Pharisees?
5. In what tangible ways did Charles Colson's ministry to prison inmates parallel Jesus's ministry to the untouchables of His day? (Look up Charles Colson's Prison Fellowship ministries online or reference one of his books as fodder for discussion.)

[30] Owen Strachan, *The Colson Way: Loving Your Neighbor and Living with Faith in a Hostile World* (Nashville: Thomas Nelson Books, 2015), 41, 45–46.

6. Have you ever been involved in a ministry to street persons, to the mentally ill, or to patients in a hospital? If so, describe a bit about your experience (e.g. the challenges and rewards and any wisdom you acquired).
7. From your conversation with other Christians in other churches, do you feel that the church is doing enough to welcome and minister to so-called "untouchables"?
8. Read the parable of the Pharisee and the tax collector (or publican) in Luke 18:9–14, and contrast the attitudes and actions of both individuals while at the temple. Do you find your own attitudes and actions (while in prayer) reflected in those of the Pharisee as well as those of the tax collector?

CHAPTER

TEN

THE INVITATION IS EXTENDED TO GENTILES

"Go out to the roads and country lanes and compel them to come in, so that my house will be full." (Luke 14:23)

"People attract other people," I was told at a church growth seminar some years ago. "The unchurched need to see something fresh and new happening in the church for them to *consider* the church." I figure that the Gentiles experienced something of this phenomena in the first century when the gospel swept in and out of towns, leaving new believers and changed lives in its afterglow. The Holy Spirit moved through the apostles' ministry, turning kingdom-outsiders into household names in the family of God. Foreigners meshed with the chosen people in a new body of the faithful woven together by the Living Word and will of God.

The parable of the great banquet reveals the heart of God for those who have yet to understand His kingdom's goods. Jesus, as the heaven-sent Son of God, demonstrated that benevolence in person. He set Israel straight by communicating that although salvation indeed came "from the Jews," they do not have exclusive claims and rights to it. Repulsive undesirables (outcasts) and resisted outsiders (Gentiles) were also on the Lord's list of invitees to the marriage feast of the Lamb.

The parable of the great banquet, then, serves as a reiteration of the promises the Lord made to Abraham—to bless the patriarch with descendants numbering something in the vicinity of the innumerable stars in the nighttime sky (see Genesis 15:5). Something Abraham couldn't have known was just how many *Gentiles* would be counted among those descendants!

English theologian Richard Bauckham notes, "In the future, when God will fulfill his promises to his own people, showing himself to be finally and definitively the gracious God they have known in their history from the Exodus onwards, God will at the same time demonstrate his deity to the nations … making his name known universally, becoming known to all as the God Israel has known."[31]

THE MYSTERY OF THE GOSPEL

In the New Testament Paul referred to the reality of Jews and Gentiles collectively making up a *single* people of faith (the church) as a mystery (a truth known only by divine revelation). This mystery was hidden in the Old Testament but has now been made known through the reconciling ministry of Christ: "This mystery is that through the gospel the Gentiles are heirs together with Israel, members together of one body, and sharers together in the promise [made to Abraham] in Christ Jesus" (Ephesians 3:6).

God wills that both Jews and Gentiles be inseparably linked and implicated in His blessings. This verse in the original Greek language renders Jews and Gentiles as joint heirs, a joint body as well as joint sharers in the promised blessings of Christ and His gospel.

As The Message version of the Bible renders it, "'God plays no favorites! It makes no difference who you are or where you're from—if you want God and are ready to do as he says, the door is open …' The believing Jews … couldn't believe that the gift of the Holy Spirit was poured out on 'outsider' non-Jews" (Acts 10:34–36, 44–46).

Paul states in Romans that "there is no difference between Jew and Gentile," in the sense that both are on the same spiritual footing when it comes to their collective need for salvation (10:12). That was explosive information in Paul's day. Jews and Gentiles were constantly at each

---

[31] Richard Bauckham, *God Crucified: Monotheism and Christology in the New Testament* (Grand Rapids: Eerdmans, 1999), 10.

other's throats, bickering and squabbling, hurting and being hurt. There was much hostility between the two groups (see Ephesians 2:14). Israel was the fattened kingdom "insider" frowning upon Gentiles. The Gentiles were the illegitimate outsiders who were encroaching on Israel's holy territory. At the temple there was an outer court made for the strict use of worshipping Gentiles. It was a provision, however, that only reinforced feelings of religious superiority and pride in the minds and hearts of Jews.

The separation of Jew from Gentile at the most holy place in Israel was quite intentional. Non-Jews were prohibited from the Jewish part of the temple under the penalty of death (see Acts 21:27–32).[32]

There was a place—albeit a perceived second-class allotment—for Gentiles at the temple, and the Jews held their noses even at that thought.

GENTILES: OUTSIDERS MADE INSIDERS!

The Jews' advantaged position before God made their perspective of the Gentiles all the more cut and dried. To be an Israelite was to be in the place of divine blessing. To be a Gentile was to be on the outside pining to be in the same spiritual shoes as the insiders (the Jews). The reasoning was that if God held Gentiles at a distance at the temple, then surely He held His covenant people of Israel all the closer. The spiritual and religious disparity that existed between Jews and Gentiles in Jesus's day—that according to Israel should've stayed carved in unalterable stone—often resulted in Jews shamelessly flaunting their elitist-like piety in front of Gentiles.

Into this divisive and discordant mix came the gospel of Jesus Christ, a gospel that incorporated Jewish *and* Gentile men and women (free and enslaved persons alike) into one body, who'd share in one Spirit, one hope, one Lord, one faith, one baptism, and one God and Father of all (see Ephesians 4:4–5). God was making more room for family around His heavenly banquet table.

The heart and will of God to see all nations and peoples, regardless of their social status and religious pedigree, become one family of God is clearly displayed in the parable of the great banquet.

After the servant informed his master that those individuals who had originally accepted an invitation to the banquet had subsequently declined,

---

[32] Craig Keener, *The IVP Bible Background Commentary: New Testament* (Downers Grove: InterVarsity Press, 2010), 101.

the master promptly instructed his servant to head in the direction of "the poor, the crippled, the blind and the lame" with banquet invitations in hand. The keen and open-hearted servant was on top of things and exclaimed to his master, "This has been already done." However, even after the socially and physically needy accepted invitations there was still much legroom left around the banquet table.

Longing to fill out the banquet he was hosting, the determined master proceeded to further instruct his servant, "Go out to the roads and country lanes and compel them to come in, so that my house will be full" (Luke 14:23).

It was a call for the servant to go outside the immediate town in order to invite a whole other group of people whom his master bid be treated as blessed insiders—and it's not like the servant *really* had to "compel them" to come to the event! (The church in the Middle Ages sometimes erroneously understood this line in the parable to condone conversions to Christianity using force and even violence if necessary.[33])

One could understand, however, why the master thought a little compelling on the part of his commissioned servant might have been in order. If those who resided outside the region of the master's mansion (along the "roads and country lanes") represent every manner of Gentile in the heathen world, then surely some would have had little to no knowledge of the God of the Jewish people.

Alfred Edersheim in *The Life and Times of Jesus the Messiah* noted,

> These wanderers on the world's highway had, before the Servant came to them, not known anything of the Master of the house, and all was quite new and unexpected. Their being invited by a Lord Whom they had not known, perhaps never heard of before, to a City in which they were strangers, and to a feast for which—as wayfarers ... they were wholly unprepared, required special urgency ... to make them either believe in it, or come to it.[34]

The principle Jesus conveys in His parable is likely one of *persuading* the spiritually lost (in this context, the Gentiles) with the gospel. By seeing the changed lives of the Lord's disciples, Gentiles would be compelled to take up God's gracious invitation for them to come and make claim

[33] Evans, *Luke*, 227.

[34] Alfred Edersheim, *The Life and Times of Jesus the Messiah* (Grand Rapids: Eerdmans, 1986 [original publication Oxford, 1886]), 251–252.

to His kingdom's eternal goods. "The phrase 'compel them to come in' does not imply that some will enter the kingdom against their will. In Palestine people politely refused an invitation until they were persuaded to accept."[35]

THE PERSUASIVE, TRANSFORMATIVE POWER OF THE GOSPEL OF JESUS CHRIST

Jesus's spectacularly unique ministry speaks for itself. Many of those who hear and observe Him in action eventually believe that He is the bridge sinners need to cross in order to get to where He came from. The Lord's soul-freeing truth and field-levelling justice and compassion indeed convict the Jew *and* Gentile alike. In no way does Jesus indulge in coercing anyone to follow Him, let alone to believe in Him as the Son of God.

John Milton, in his classic *Paradise Lost,* stated, "Who overcomes by force, hath overcome but half his foe." Milton's epic work discusses the heavenly battle between good and evil, God and Satan. In the course of the devil's cunning endeavours to overtake the souls of humans, he ends up causing both the spiritual downfall of humanity and the eternal damnation of himself and his fellow comrades in wickedness—the fallen angels. In a heaven versus hell war for the souls of humanity, Milton's aforementioned words could also apply to how the gospel has been stuffed down the throats of unbelievers at times throughout the history of Christian world missions. Winning souls by drawn sword, the threat of death, and even imprisonment was never Jesus's approach to fulfilling the Great Commission!

Jesus's Great Commission to His church is based on eternal spiritual truth and the persuasive power of the Holy Spirit to save and wholly transform lives. God's desire is for *us* to say "Yes" to His goodness and grace—minus any arm-twisting on His part! God's ultimate aim is to have those whom He redeems become aligned with the matchless and transcendent values of the kingdom His Son launched at His incarnation.

Christianity's spread has had a greater impact on society than any other movement in the history of human existence. The early signs of this are evident in and through the one-of-a-kind person and ministry of Jesus Christ. Helpless, hopeless sinners who crave unconditional love find

[35] *The Baker Illustrated Bible Commentary*, eds. Gary M. Burge and Andrew E. Hill (Grand Rapids: BakerBooks), 1090.

it embodied in the God-man who came to them directly from the majestic confines of heaven itself. Jesus comes to love and befriend *all* manner of people. The Gospel accounts capture the Lord's close affinity with those who were branded misfits, social outcasts, and outsiders in His day.

Gentiles who put their faith in Jesus understood that in Him God was offering them a way back from the dark paths of religious ignorance and sin. Gentiles were not somehow in the salvation picture all of a sudden; they were *meant* to come into His kingdom!

The parable of the great banquet, then, was also intended by the Lord to educate the unbelieving Jews on the vastness and inclusiveness of God's saving grace, as prophesied by Isaiah. "Surely you will summon nations you know not, and nations that do not know you will come running to you" (Isaiah 55:5). And again in Isaiah 56:3, "Let no foreigner who is bound to the LORD say, 'The LORD will surely exclude me from his people.'"

THE INVITATIONAL BLESSING OF THE GENTILES

The servant in the parable of the great banquet becomes what Israel was commanded by Yahweh to be: a witness to the Gentiles. God always intended to enlarge the tent of His chosen people (indeed His banquet table as well) by adding to them nations outside of Israel (see Matthew 8:11). Jesus alludes to "other sheep" outside of His own (Israel) needing to be brought into the pen of His shepherding care (John 10:16). Commenting on Isaiah 42:6, Barry Webb states, "The God who made the world is committed to its welfare … there is a 'covenant' between God and the human race … the Servant, as a covenant for the people and a light for the Gentiles, is to be the very embodiment of that covenant."[36]

The Lord does not allow the self-righteous to complain when He invites the straying and lowly sinner and, in the case of the parable of the great banquet, even Gentiles to dine with Him at the marriage feast of the Lamb. Israel's bungled messianic expectations concerning Jesus ignored the promise God made to Abraham that "all peoples" would be "blessed" through him (see Genesis 12:1–13). At the expense of unbelieving Israel, nations outside of it would be given the opportunity to gain glad access into the grace of God and secure a place around His banquet table!

[36] Barry G. Webb, *The Message of Isaiah,* The Bible Speaks Today, ed. J. A. Motyer (Downer's Grove: IVP Academic, 1996), 171–172.

Those who were reputed to be outsiders in Jesus's day were invited to revel in the glint of His kingdom's mercy, a kingdom that was now within their reach, where they'd go to bask in its full glow for eternity. Disdained outsiders now had an inside track on the grace of God! Call them Gentiles; call them non-Jews; call them grateful outlaws, outliers, and outsiders. What we will not be able to call them—is late for the banquet dinner!

REFLECTIVE QUESTIONS

1. It's always been God's plan to break down the "wall of hostility" between Jews and Gentiles by making them into one body and family of faith (Ephesians 2:14). Why do you think some Jews were jealous of Gentiles being blessed by God and graciously brought under the covenant blessings He promised to Israel?
2. Have you ever been jealous or envious of God blessing other believers in ways you've longed to be blessed—especially if you felt you were overlooked or more deserving?
3. Most of us, at one time or another, have felt like an "outsider." Describe the setting and background and the feeling you had.
4. Put yourself in the shoes of a Gentile—how might you have felt when going to the temple to worship, knowing you were segregated from the Jews worshipping there?
5. The Bible tells us that we'll see people of every tribe, language, and nation in heaven (Revelation 5:9). How often do you ponder that fact? Does it influence your interest in supporting or participating in missions?
6. In what ways might the church be perceived as being an isolationist entity?
7. The book of Acts shows us that Gentiles were often more open to the apostles' teaching on Jesus than the Jews were. What do you think the Gentile nations saw in the apostles' ministry and heard about Jesus that stirred their hearts towards accepting Him?
8. Although God loves all people, the parable of the great banquet (and indeed the Gospels and the entire Bible) attests to the fact that He has an especially compassionate concern for the outcast and outsider (e.g. the blind, poor, sick, oppressed). In what ways should this inform the ministry initiatives of the church and the testimony of Christians?

9. Do you think that cultures that have little to no knowledge of who Jesus is may be easier to evangelize than those already possessing a basic understanding of His ministry?
10. Using your knowledge of history, other religions, and the Bible, reflect on the tangible ways Christianity has made a unique contribution and perhaps the greatest impact on society and the world.

CHAPTER

ELEVEN

HOPE: A SECOND CHANCE FOR ISRAEL TO RSVP

Hope is a precious human commodity. Believers all over the world possess a uniquely collective hope in the return of the Saviour from heaven. No amount of opposition, personal failure, or setbacks in the spiritual life can cancel out the certain promise of God to redeem His people and bring them into His eternal kingdom, a people comprised of both Christians and Jewish believers in Christ. One glorious day, all believers will reap the inheritance of their faith in the Son of God.

Thanks to the ministry of the prophets, Israel could also cling to the promises of a better day—in a word: hope!

The incorrigible nature of Israel often rendered the nation the object and project of divine reclamation. Instead of forgetting about them, Yahweh was faithful to them. Instead of wiping them out, He wrangled them back into His protective bosom time and time again. They belong to Him! Regardless of the judgments God had periodically brought against them, regardless of their lengthy resumé of spiritual infractions and a hidebound approach to obeying God, Israel remained His treasured possession. A trek through the prophetic books of the Old Testament reveals God's longsuffering love for His people. He desired to turn the

Israelites from a prodigal people in exile into a nation for His praise and glory.

God had always kept a remnant of His people for Himself whom He sought to bless, right up to the time when their promised redeemer would satisfy their longings for revival and redemption. Throughout generations, Israel possessed this hope amid the testing gales of national and spiritual uncertainty. Their invitation to the expected messianic feast in the last day was airmailed to them from heaven in the person and ministry of Jesus of Nazareth.

Hope is God's calling card for those among a prodigal Israel who accept His Son, even at the eleventh hour. Jesus has always been a sanctuary for some and yet a "stone" causing those who are offended by Him to stumble (see Isaiah 8:14; 1 Peter 2:7–8). The Lord informed the religious leaders that even if His followers keep silent in their praise of Him, "the stones will cry out" in their stead (Luke 19:40). Stones, rocks, and worship are symbolically linked together in Scripture. Consider the building of altars in the Old Testament. Altars were platform-like structures made of rocks, upon which sacrificial offerings were made to the Lord. Altars were also constructed as a means of witnessing to the goodness and faithfulness of God. And in no other way is that goodness and faithfulness more visible than in the saving, gracious altar that is His Son, Jesus Christ.

ISRAEL AND THE ETERNAL PLAN OF GOD

Since His advent into the world, a stone the size of the third person of the Trinity has been laid at the spiritual feet of Israel, and that stone is not going anywhere anytime soon. The Jewish people—like every other nation and peoples under heaven—can continue to stumble over this stone, or they can fall at its feet and worship with a sacrifice of praise to the rock of their salvation, Jesus.

The Lord's message in the parable of the great banquet, coupled with the current spiritual state of Israel, which lingers in its unbelief, gives rise to the question as to whether there is any hope for the Jewish people to accept Jesus as their Messiah. If God's covenantal blessings are ultimately fulfilled in His Son and if the Jewish people continue in their course of dismissing Him as their promised deliverer, where does that leave them? Eternity is a long time to be wrong about Jesus Christ!

Thankfully, the Bible assures us that all is *not* lost for the people of Israel. This is why the Jewish people, despite their long history of rejecting any thought of embracing Christ as their nation's Messiah and king, remain in the redemption conversation! The Jewish people have not crossed the Rubicon of unbelief to the point where they're left without a chance of rebounding and landing on the side of salvation. Led along by the Holy Spirit, the apostle Paul expressed to the believers in Rome (a largely Gentile church) the hope he held out for his fellow Jews: "Did God reject his people? By no means! … And if they do not persist in unbelief, they will be grafted in, for God is able to graft them in again" (Romans 11:1, 23).

The root meaning of the word *graft* in the original Greek *egkentrizo* is "to prick or puncture—as in making a puncture to graft a living shoot (branch) into another living plant (tree)." The six forms of *egkentrizo* in the New Testament all occur in Romans 11:17–24 and always refer to God combining His two redeemed groups (Jews and Gentile believers) into one.

The Psalms contain prophetic prayers of hope that Israel will awaken from its unbelief in the Saviour of the world. Here is a petition to the Lord for Him to show favour towards the Davidic king (fulfilled in Jesus Christ) as the Lord's anointed (Israel's redeemer), who is seated in the place of honour in God's presence: "Let your hand rest on the man at your right hand, the son of man you have raised up for yourself. Then we will not turn away from you; revive us, and we will call on your name. Restore us, LORD God Almighty; make your face shine on us, that we may be saved" (Psalm 80:17–19).

One day many among Israel will realize their transgression against God in rejecting their Messiah. At that time, God will fuse them like a branch into a life-giving vine that's ripe with the promises the Lord made to Abraham, via the imputed righteousness of Jesus Christ. Until then, the Jewish people's worship of their God will remain misdirected, incomplete, and ultimately unfulfilling. This was knowledge Paul and his missionary companions were bent on dispensing to their unbelieving fellow Jews.

The foundations of Israel's spiritual atrophy had long been laid of course by the time Paul and his *leave-no-Jew-behind* gospel crusade hit the trails of Asia and points beyond. Despite the barricades of defiance many of the unbelieving Jews constructed that made the penetration of the gospel into Gentile regions an exhausting venture, and despite his enemies' scare tactics, Paul refused to be silent when it came to preaching Christ to his fellow Israelites.

The determined apostle was set aflame evangelistically by the truth that "what is impossible with man is possible with God" (Luke 18:27); for even he, Paul, a once irascibly legalistic Pharisee, was brought to his humbled knees and made to confess that Jesus is Lord (see Acts 9:1–5; Philippians 2:10–11)! It made perfect sense, then, for Paul to be the one to bring the gospel to the Jews; that is, until they bounced the apostle from every synagogue they found him in with an aim to ultimately "deep-six" him along with his pro-Jesus messages.

EVANGELIZING JEWS WITH THE GOSPEL

A recent statement from the Vatican seems to contradict the fact that theological differences actually exist between Jews and Christians.

> From the Christian confession that there can be only one path to salvation, however, it does not in any way follow that the Jews are excluded from God's salvation because they do not believe Jesus Christ as the Messiah of Israel and the Son of God … In concrete terms this means that the Catholic Church neither conducts nor supports any specific institutional mission work directed towards Jews.[37]

Positions like these find a formidable challenge in the evangelical branch of Jesus's church. Passages in Matthew 28, Acts 1:8, and even Romans 1:16 are difficult for evangelicals to ignore in terms of their stimulus and justification for worldwide evangelism (including gospel ministries to Jewish people). Even Jewish believers have long been cognizant of the need for concerted evangelistic efforts in reaching their fellow Jews with the gospel of Christ.

For example, Jews for Jesus (JFJ), founded in 1981, is an evangelistic agency dedicated to bringing the gospel to places where a "significant Jewish testimony is needed." The organization explains, "Jewish people

[37] "'The Gifts and the Calling of God Are Irrevocable' (Rom 11:29): A Reflection on Theological Questions Pertaining to Catholic-Jewish Relations on the Occasion of the 50th Anniversary of 'Nostra Aetate' (No. 4)," Commission for Religious Relations with the Jews (December 10, 2015), 36, 40.

tend to dismiss evangelistic methods and materials that are couched in Christian presuppositions and lingo, because they reinforce the assumption that Jesus is for 'them' not 'us.' In order to get beyond that assumption, we have to be innovative."[38] Consequently, JFJ strives to communicate the gospel with the use of creative avenues such as humour-laden evangelistic literature, music and drama, witnessing campaigns, secular media outreach, and internet ministry.

The banquet invitations that the servant in Jesus's parable distributed on behalf of his master to those who were to be the first to come in and first to be served (Israel) become for us as Christ's ambassadors the very gospel we're called to persuade unbelieving Jews with. Communicating our case for Christ to a Jewish person is an exercise needing to be soaked in preparatory prayer and the Word of God. It's a daunting mission, to be sure. However, with the Holy Spirit charging our efforts, it's also one that's not entirely impossible to fulfill! God is simply calling us as the church to engage our Jewish friends on the redemptive ground and expectation we share: that of Israel's yearning for Messiah to come and Christians' groaning for their Saviour to come again.

HOPE FOR ISRAEL

The Bible tells us that a spiritually revived and reawakened remnant of Israel will turn from its rejection of Jesus Christ and reign with their Messiah after He conquers the enemies of God (see Ezekiel 38–39; Zechariah 8:7–8, 12:8–9, 14:3–4; Romans 11:1–5; Revelation 7:1–8, 20:7–10).

Jesus is very clear: not everyone is going to heaven (see Matthew 7:13–14). Not everyone is going to sit and dine with the exalted Lamb at His heavenly marriage feast. There's a prohibitive bar across the entranceway into heaven, as it were. Though we don't read of a literal one in the Bible, make no mistake; one *does* exist—if only because heaven's alternative does; to miss out on the one (heaven) guarantees our eternal placement in the other (hell). God doesn't want it to be this way. He takes no pleasure in the eternal death and suffering of human lives and souls. That is why He sent His Son to us!

At present there remain unclaimed seats around the banquet table of heaven that will eventually be filled by every last Jewish believer in Christ.

[38] See http://jewsforjesus.ca/what-we-do.

Despite the chord of finality the master strums with his statement in the parable of the great banquet that "not one of those who were invited will get a taste of my banquet," there *is* hope for Israel.

In eternity, when we're rejoicing in the kingdom of God, the present earthly distinctions we make between Jews and Gentiles will no longer exist—only saved worshippers of Jesus Christ will be there!

REFLECTIVE QUESTIONS

1. Share any discussions you may have had with Jews regarding your faith in Jesus Christ. How did they respond? Was any common spiritual ground established?
2. Why might evangelizing Jews be more difficult than sharing Jesus with individuals from other religions?
3. What thoughts come to mind when you consider that a remnant of people within Israel will eventually accept Christ as their Messiah?
4. What do you think Paul meant when he said "all Israel will be saved" (Romans 11:26)?
5. What is your response to the Roman Catholic Church's claim that Jews needn't be evangelized?
6. Organizations such as Jews for Jesus (JFJ) possess a deep conviction for reaching unbelieving Jewish people with the gospel. Using the methodology of JFJ as a guide, what are some ways that churches situated among a Jewish population could have a ministry to the chosen people?

CHAPTER

TWELVE

THE SERVANT IN THE PARABLE OF THE GREAT BANQUET

"At the time of the banquet [the master] sent his servant to tell those who had been invited, 'Come, for everything is now ready.'" (Luke 14:17)

Perhaps you've heard someone say "As long as you're breathing, God can use you." We learn from Scripture that every child of God is a servant of God. We may be able to have two feet in the kingdom without serving it, but we cannot claim to have a spiritually productive or obedient faith if deeds of service are noticeably absent from it (James 2:26). Salvation and service go hand in hand. If anyone taught and modelled that to perfection, it was Jesus. Perhaps the ideal servant might have the attitude "Anywhere, anytime, anyhow You need me, Lord, just call!" Such an outlook on serving God is certainly admirable, even if somewhat unrealistic. A better definition of a servant may well be one who simply offers "I'm willing and available, Lord. Just use me." The servant in Jesus's parable of the great banquet personifies one who does the bidding of a king, one who knows the challenges involved with serving a kingdom and yet does exactly what his master asks of him—and does it well.

By all accounts, the seminal church kept in spiritual step with the Lord's characteristically servant-hearted ministry. The early Christians willingly carried on with a gospel that was breaking down barriers of paganism and unbelief and taking residence in the hearts of Jews and Gentiles alike, a gospel inviting sinners to heed the grace and mercy of God in Jesus Christ and compelling them to come into His kingdom and feast at His banquet. That same gospel invitation still beckons lost sinners today, and God is still calling and commissioning servants to serve Him by taking the Good News wherever they trod.

Perhaps the most well-travelled and well-loved, not to mention one of the most *fruitful* servants to come along over the past century, was the late Billy Graham. God chose a farm boy from out of Charlotte, North Carolina, to preach to millions upon millions of people. Graham would go on to minister to politicians and presidents in the United States and notable figures around the world. On many occasions leaders who were influenced by Graham's shining testimony would ask him questions about God and religion.

The question needing to be answered by all human beings is whether they can be sure they will make it to heaven. President Lyndon Johnson ("LBJ") once asked Graham, "Will I see my parents when I die?"[39] Johnson was stuck and sinking deeper still in the muskeg that was the immensely unpopular Vietnam War in the 1960s. With the mounting deaths of American servicemen and women streaming forth like a parade of endless sorrow through his conscience, and with the inescapable reality of his own human finitude as an elderly president bound up in his thoughts, Johnson needed much more than the assurance of temporal peace and hope. On one of Graham's visits to Johnson's ranch in Texas, Johnson "asked Graham to share the gospel with him once again."[40]

In and through his service to the kingdom of God Billy Graham touched hearts and lives across every continent with the gospel of Jesus Christ. In essence, the activity of the servant in Jesus's parable of the great banquet parallels what Billy Graham sought to accomplish in his ministry as an ambassador for Christ and His gospel.

[39] Nancy Gibbs and Michael Duffy, *The Preacher and the Presidents: Billy Graham in the White House* (New York: Center Street Publishing, 2008), xi.
[40] David Cohen, "Billy Graham, Influential Evangelist and Friend to U.S. Presidents, Dies at 99," *Politico*, February 21, 2018.

THE SERVANT OF LUKE 14:17

In Scripture, Israel is referred to as the Lord's servant (Isaiah 41:8–9, 49:3). The Bible also identifies Isaiah's "servant" as being the divine person of Christ in His messianic role (see Isaiah 42:1–7). In the royal terminology of the ancient Near East, *servant* could mean something like "trusted envoy" or "confidential representative." In other words, the nature of Isaiah's servant could be understood as one tending to the commands of a king: Yahweh (Israel's God and preeminent leader). As the righteous, incarnated God-man and Saviour of the world, Jesus remains the sole bringer of justice to the nations. As *the* Servant, Christ is the one who came to open the eyes of the blind, free captives, release from the dungeon those who sit in darkness, and ultimately gather Israel to Himself (see Isaiah 42:6–7, 49:5; see also Luke 4:18–19; Matthew 20:28).

In the Lord's day, a servant was also understood in slave vernacular as someone who was the property of his master and the submissive hands and feet at his bidding—a role describing the Son of God's *seeking*, *serving, saving,* and *sending* ministry to a tee! (See Mark 10:45; Luke 19:10; John 3:17, 5:17, 6:44, 14:6, 20:21.)

It would stand to reason, then, that it is largely accepted within scholarly circles that the benevolent master in Jesus's parable of the great banquet is representative of the first person of the Holy Trinity—God the Father. With that view in mind, we can understand the identity of the servant in the parable as the incarnated Son of God, *the* servant who was charged with searching out those whom His Father in heaven bids to invite to the marriage feast of the Lamb.

The Gospels also speak of *Jesus* being His disciples' master, who authorizes, empowers, and commissions them to serve Him in His kingdom work. Matthew 28:18–20, commonly referred to as "the Great Commission," forms the basis for Christian evangelism and missions. It was Jesus's parting post-resurrection instruction to His followers to spread His teachings around the world and to baptize those who believed in the names of the Trinity. It is a wonderful blueprint for reaching and growing people with the gospel, to be sure, despite the fact that God's people tend to have difficulty living it out!

However, Jesus is clear about the fact that servants of God *serve!* And it's not like He didn't practice what He commanded of us. Our Lord left us with examples of how His message was authenticated through His sacrificial service to sinners even as He sought them. Like the servant in the parable of the great banquet who was commissioned to search high and low for those his master sought to bring into his banquet, Jesus went all out in order to communicate the benevolent character of His Father and His kingdom to the spiritually lost. This is what He's called His church to accomplish! As evidenced by the content of various New Testament letters, this challenge was embraced by the Christians and churches throughout Asia Minor.

SERVING THE GOSPEL IN THE EARLY CHURCH

Following in the servant-hearted footsteps of *the* Servant of God Himself (Christ) was something the first Christians appear to have been both good and faithful at. Fresh from their commissioning, Jesus's disciples likely hadn't put it all together in terms of *how* they were to move from possessing a framework for evangelism and discipleship to actually constructing their Master's church.

However, not long after the Lord ascended back into heaven, the apostles and other believers in the early church understood *why* their Master Jesus conferred such high objectives on them. Just as Jesus said would happen, His followers became supernaturally enabled by the ministry of the promised Holy Spirit to effectually salt and light up their world (see Matthew 5:13–16). Before the church (and Christianity in general) had a chance to gain favourable traction within the Roman Empire, it was already climbing in membership and spreading in influence.

Luke, in the book of Acts, makes us aware that the early believers made an indelible impression upon the communities around them (see Acts 2:47). Undoubtedly their servant-hearted ministries of charitable giving and healing, among other manifestations of God's grace, were impactful components. The apostles accepted the hospitality of God-fearers, seekers, and skeptics alike, and by spending time with them they left various homes and families lit by the saving light of the gospel (10:26–48, 16:11–15, 31–34).

After Jewish persecution struck their home base of Jerusalem, the early believers—with the same unction the servant in Jesus's parable of the great banquet exercised—took their Lord's commission upon their servants' shoulders and carried it, like Billy Graham would centuries later, to the kings and kingdoms and powers and populace of their day. Lost souls were being eternally saved and tallied in heaven's ledger, while crops of new believers streamed into the already inflating assemblies of the church. Lives that had been deeply indoctrinated in the league of nebulous Roman deities were being freed to know and serve the one true living God in Christ!

Evangelism in the early church doesn't appear to have been practised as a passive exercise of the believers' faith or with a "wait until the unbelieving come to us" attitude. The early followers of Jesus were the antithesis of the evangelistic wariness that has largely overtaken the North American church today. The believers in Acts appear to have been able to demonstrate the often-heard platitude within modern Christian culture that the church ought to minister as though it has no "walls." Their service to Christ didn't amount to simply preaching about Him; it also involved concerted efforts to *be* Jesus to their society. The people of the Way were not solely people "of the Word" but also people of that Word's fruit.

Many in the pioneer church of Jesus Christ took Jesus wherever they trod. They were walking, talking, living, and breathing gospel tracts. As hungry soul-harvesters they lined up to play the role of the servant in the real-life production of the parable of the great banquet! The early believers grasped that just as invitations to banquets were made to be given out to invitees, so also their knowledge of a life-changing and eternity-altering God in Jesus Christ begged to be shared among those to whom the Saviour sent them!

AN AGES-OLD AND CONTINUING CALL TO KINGDOM SERVANTHOOD

Ages before a converted Mosaic-Law geek and former persecutor of Christians named Paul (formerly known as Saul of Tarsus) made it vogue in the early church, the ancient Israelites were called to be servant-lights to the Gentiles (see Genesis 12:1–3; Isaiah 49:6). Operation World Redemption commenced with the calling of a couple of geriatrics—Abraham and, later, Moses—who from a twenty-first century perspective should've been gearing up for their long-overdue retirement parties, not given leading roles and faith-stretching assignments from the Lord!

That same call was transmitted through a kaleidoscope of persons in the form of Israel's monarchs, priests, and prophets, culminating in the coming of God's promised redeemer, Jesus Christ, whose subsequent calling of apostles and every manner of disciple contributed to the ministry of the Jerusalem church in the first century.

As the time for our Lord's return draws ever nearer, God's call to His church couldn't be any more urgent: to invite—in word and in deed—the spiritually lost to consider partaking of the banquet of truth and everlasting life embodied in the person of His Son, Jesus Christ. It's an invitation back to the garden of righteous communion with the living God, an invitation for the unsaved to escape the hook of eternal judgment and let Jesus answer to Almighty God for their sin.

Since the first act of rebellion in the Garden of Eden, God has been revealing His gracious heart to sinners and calling them back to Him. He continues to call and to enable willing servants to press on with His quest to demonstrate and disseminate the beautiful invitation of the gospel in their *Jerusalems, Samarias, Judeas, and ends of the earth* (see Acts 1:8).

REFLECTIVE QUESTIONS

1. Taking Billy Graham as one example, what spiritual qualities and attributes did he seem to possess that made him such an effective servant of God? Do you see some of the same attributes in your life?
2. In what ways does the servant in Jesus's parable of the great banquet resemble the Lord's ministry in the Gospels?
3. Do you view your calling as a servant of Christ's gospel as potentially dangerous?
4. Why is serving others such a challenging facet of the spiritual life at times? Do you think our culture views servanthood in a more negative or positive manner?
5. In what tangible ways can we serve God day to day as "salt" and "light"?
6. What kinds of things could we as Jesus's church in the twenty-first century learn from the early church's living out of their faith? In what ways might the church today be more capable in personal and corporate evangelism?
7. What do you feel might be the greatest obstacle keeping you from becoming more of the evangelistic servant in word and deed that God wants you to be?

CHAPTER THIRTEEN

THE SERVANT'S LAMENT

"Please excuse me … I can't come." (Luke 14:18–20)

When we retrace the steps of loneliness the Saviour often walked, the common denominator in most of those situations boils down to His ministry being rejected in one form or another. Whether Jesus was escaping through murderous crowds, was told to hit the road, or moved on from regions where He couldn't even do miracles, He knew rejection like a book He had read several times cover to cover.

I've always found the Gospel accounts of the triumphal entry to represent the most galvanizing image of the rejection of Jesus Christ—that is, if we observe it from the *Lord's* perspective. As He rode into Jerusalem on a donkey, many of Jesus's followers and fair-weather fans were expecting Him—if He was indeed the promised Messiah and the one who'd sit on David's throne—to cause an uprising of wrathful and apocalyptic proportions against their hated overlord, the Roman Empire. No longer would God's people be subjected to taking orders from centurions. Their hopes and dreams of a restored kingdom of Israel could finally take flight. Besides, unlike in times past, Jesus, as He sat atop His donkey-sized throne, was no longer hushing the throngs cheering

His earthly coronation. They knew the Messiah would finally arrive to rescue God's chosen people, just as the prophets had been predicting for centuries.

Everything about the scene looked favourable to the nation of Israel. But as we follow Luke's storyline of Jesus's triumphal entry into Jerusalem, what doesn't seem to belong are the tears that were welling up in His divine eyes and streaming down His pained face.

In Bible history, divine grief has spoken through a catastrophic flood, through famines, and through the foes of God's people. As Jesus approached Jerusalem one final time on His way to the cross, the grief of God spoke once again, this time through the moist eyes of His Son. Jesus's tears were hardly tears of joy, as if He could be fooled into believing that Israel had conclusively thrown the weight of their faith behind Him. The tears of Jesus, rather, spoke of a divine sadness that only a Roman crossbeam and an expired second person of the Trinity could give perspective to. Never mind Balaam's donkey, this time God was speaking through the one weeping *on* the donkey!

The sinless Son of God refused to use any leverage He might've garnered from the spectacle to engage in a little payback at the expense of His flummoxed detractors. The account of the triumphal entry shows a Saviour unwilling to induce the maximum outrage of the religious leaders looking on. We don't read of Jesus winking with smugness at the ego-bruised Pharisees and issuing them a patronizing "I told you so. *I am* God—and that means *you* lost!" The Lord chose not to rub His popularity in the faces of a contingent of Pharisees who were grousing and demanding that the controversial and yet much-celebrated rabbi silence His blasphemous followers' deafening praise of Him (see Luke 19:39). The religious leaders had sown seeds of enmity with the Lord and had drawn their lines for battling Him; now, the masses' worship of the Nazarene tugged all the more at their fury.

The Lord, on the other hand, seemed not the least bit impressed by the crowd brandishing palm fronds and celebrating His entrance into Jerusalem. He knew better than anyone that the praises of God's people were conditional and could change like quicksilver. It may have been the beginning of a Passover like none other, promising a heightened sense of messianic hopes and national dreams coming true, yet Jesus had Good

Friday on His mind. It may have been the Saviour's party, but He'd cry at it if He wanted to—and He did.

The Lord knew He was penetrating a city prepped for His demise and a people primed for turning their backs on Him and the executioner's cross they'd have Him nailed to. It would be personal rejection at its worst! An undercurrent of malfeasance ran beneath the ultimately empty praises He heard along the path. Despite the due honour He was receiving, Jesus entered the holy city and centre of Jewish worship as God visibly dismayed over the spiritually tragic state of His prodigal people's hearts.

THE PARABLE OF THE LOST SON

One of the most riveting and contemplative parables is the one referred to as the lost son in Luke 15. In the parable, the younger of two sons trades in his silver spoon (his inheritance) for what turns out to be a heaping helping of reality! We think that if anyone got what they deserved it was this naive whippersnapper who was living the "life of Riley" under his old man's roof. At his son's request, the father gave his youngest lad his rightful portion of the estate's worth.

With his pockets bulging with currency, the young man struck out on his own. The love, security, and blessed position he enjoyed in his father's home suddenly seemed inferior to the rising aroma of wild oats just waiting to be sown from afar!

The parable of the lost son in many respects mirrors the history of Israel's prodigal nature and subsequent rejection of their Messiah. The Israelites had no peer among the inhabitants of the neighbouring nations. They enjoyed "backstage pass" status, as it were, in having intimate access to Yahweh, who "revealed his word … his laws and decrees" to them—something He did for "no other nation" (Psalm 147:19–20). They were the apple of their God's eye and "treasured" as His very "possession" (Exodus 19:5).

The Israelites had it made under the wing of their God's protection and provision. Wouldn't you think that a people who were rescued by God out of slavery, who were led through a land of many enemies and brought safely into a land flowing with milk and honey and the richest of agricultural fare, would in turn be faithful to Him? Na ah! That's not what happened with the nation of Israel.

Instead, they pulled a prodigal son and squandered the good faith of their God. Israel's final act of spiritual treachery and unbelief culminated in their demand that the Son of God be crucified. If any word captures the response Jesus received to His pronouncements that the kingdom of God had come with Him and that reservations were being made for the great marriage feast of the Lamb, it's *rejection!*

The servant in the parable of the great banquet too came face-to-face with the cost of rejection. When he announced that his master's banquet was ready to receive those who had previously been invited, his good news fell on heedless ears. The servant surely lamented the three excuses he received from people he surely thought would've made their hurried way to the grand event. The servant felt the bullets of rejection to his master's kind banquet invitations before his master ever did. And a servant who respected his master and enjoyed his favour could very well have taken anything that affected *him* to heart.

ENCOUNTERING REJECTION

When I was pastoring a church plant, our leadership implemented a highly affordable (and high quality, I might add) monthly dinner as a ministry to the immediate community. The meal was often accompanied by music and other stimulating media. These events were attended primarily by people from a needy economic bracket. Those who were on a more financially comfortable plane, however, who generously contributed to the operation of the meal, showed little to no interest in accepting our church's invitation to attend the event, even after expressing their interest in attending!

Over time, I couldn't help but wonder whether the more well-to-do crowd had something better to do than to participate in a meal that reached out to and fed the less fortunate. Perhaps being invited to the dinners was an insult to the more well off in the community. Perhaps it was a pride issue. Perhaps they couldn't or *wouldn't* see their need to be ministered to. Although I spent much time in prayer trying to process the matter, it felt like those whom we had first extended God's welcome and blessing to, who had accepted the need for and helped support the ministry, repeatedly rejected our goodwill.

At such times we can take solace in the fact that Jesus can relate. No one has ever experienced rejection quite like the Son of God. His underappreciated ministry provided ample reason for reading between the lines of His burden for the spiritually lost. As Isaiah prophesied, Jesus, as the Servant of God, experienced enormous suffering (even excruciating physical suffering on the cross), in addition to rejection and personal pain throughout His public ministry years (Isaiah 53:3–9). That reality alone should tell us that reaching those without Christ is an exercise loaded with possibilities for experiencing relational hazards and personal rejection.

The Saviour was upfront about the perils and pitfalls intertwined with one's decision to follow Him. If devilish opposition is a given danger lurking on the perimeters of the Great Commission, then experiencing rejection while witnessing for Christ is a risk that shouldn't take the child of God by surprise either. It's hard sometimes not to take an unbeliever's "No" as a hard-to-swallow dose of personal rejection. The invitation we issue our unsaved friends to attend a church service, a Bible study for "seekers," or some outreach initiative are often met with a ten-foot pole of chilliness, and the rejection can have a thorny effect by how it rips at our burden for their souls.

What evangelistically inclined Christian hasn't experienced at least one occasion when someone adamantly communicated —perhaps with a few expletives thrown in for added effect—that they were not at all interested in what Christians have to share about Jesus? It can seem at times like people without the Lord get to reject our good intentions while those who only want to make Him known get to have headaches! It's hard not to feel at times like Christians are paying their servant dues for a chance at singing the evangelist's blues!

Whenever the name that is above all other names—the name of Jesus—is disparaged, the disciple of Christ feels a blow. Sometimes those blows land with the thud of suffering. Although a servant-oriented and servant-hearted lifestyle is undoubtedly a God-glorifying one, the history of Christianity stands to remind us of the challenges as well as dangers involved in saying "Yes" to Jesus and His commissioning of our lives as His disciples and servants. Unfortunately, the prospect of rejection goes hand in hand with the privilege of serving the kingdom of God!

OPPOSITION TO THE GOSPEL IS A GIVEN

The Lord always knew how to deliver a statement for pure shock value. There were other times, however, when Jesus was just stating facts, when He was just keeping things "real." One of those occasions was when He likened His commissioning of the disciples to sending them out as vulnerable mutton into realms where awaiting packs of big bad gospel-hostile wolves trod (see Matthew 10:16). Peter's scheming and dreaming at Jesus's transfiguration was proof enough that the disciples needed periodic doses of the realities surrounding their identification with a suffering Saviour and, still to come, a great and yet challenging and opposition-ridden commission. Numerous times the Son of God sought to impress upon His closest disciples that the one who saved them and called them to serve Him was asking them to do so knowing that it would never be entirely safe for them.

The Lord was saying that when it comes to exercising their Great Commission legs, His disciples must be aware that responses to their evangelistic ministry could bite with wolfish and even deadly intent. Scripture educates us that there's an unseen and yet very real (and evil) entity pulling the strings of earthly opposition against God's people. The Holy Spirit led Peter to describe Satan as a prowling lion whose modus operandi is to do what lions naturally do—hunt down their prey—and destroy the lives of Christ followers (1 Peter 5:8)! Not everyone who rejects our overtures with the gospel will physically harm us, of course. Yet any form of rejection on account of Christ is never easy to encounter, let alone digest.

Nonetheless, our Lord's sending of His church into the world is neither limited to nor threatened by any amount of rejection or negative response to the gospel. Our ultimate goal as Christ followers is to persevere in faithfulness for the sake of His call, glory, and kingdom. Every lost sinner saved counts for eternity and gets heaven rejoicing. Seeing redeemed lives added to the pews of Jesus's heavenly sanctuary is well worth risking rejection from the unsaved.

That being said, let's be real. Being an ambassador for Jesus is *not* a convenient calling; it's difficult even on the best of days. Presenting a polarizing Saviour to the average twenty-first-century person can cause anxiety levels to spike within even the most evangelistically gifted Christians. Words that believers use within Christian culture (e.g. *sacrifice, sin, repentance,* and *obedience*) have all but disappeared from the vocabulary and conscience of our postmodern, post-Christian society.

Our Lord, however, never seemed to employ soft words in order to make hard spiritual arguments. He was brutal in His honesty. Jesus knew that hell-produced lies will always sound more soothing to the ears of sinners than hurtful truths that lead to eternal life.

The Saviour made clear His expectations of all who'd declared their allegiance to Him (see Luke 9:57–62). Neither their profession of faith *in* Him nor their commitment *to* Him was to be characteristically shallow. There would be much that would test His disciples' allegiance to Him, much that would stretch their faithfulness. Challenges to their will to keep going along with the Lord would sprout serious legs. Jesus is Lord of all, and those who followed Him had to be "all in." In fact, they were to be prepared to lose all they had—even their very lives—for merely being seen with Jesus, let alone for having openly called Him "Lord"!

As fulfilling and spiritually rewarding as our faith relationship with Christ can be—and ultimately will be in eternity—following Him in the here and now comes with a string of cost attached. We cannot be a Jesus follower without being willing, as Jesus was, to bear a cross of self-denial and rejection. For disciples of Christ, then, it's not a matter of *if* but rather *when* we will be rejected on account of our identification with a suffering Saviour.

WALKING IN THE FOOTSTEPS OF A REJECTED JESUS

The Son of God never got to walk down easy street during His earthly ministry; consequently, neither will those who choose to "take up their cross" and follow in His footsteps be able to avoid tests to their discipleship (Luke 9:23). The rejections our Lord experienced that brought about unjust suffering in His life are transferred to those who bear the name of Jesus in the world (see Philippians 1:29).

In other words, God's people must be ready and willing to go without, do without, and even be put out on account of their commitment and service to the Saviour. The fifteenth century Dutch Catholic mystic Thomas à Kempis called this simply living the "Jesus life."

Author Steven James explains, "To Thomas, the 'Jesus life' is one of faith rather than sight, simplicity rather than extravagance, moderation rather than indulgence, sacrifice rather than acquisition, and risking the ways of God rather than settling into the soul-numbing security of the ways of the world."[41]

One could suppose that attempting to live as Jesus did is universally viewed as a noble thing to do. Not many cultures or religious belief systems, even if they reject the teachings of Christianity, could dispute that. It's when Christians begin to talk about Jesus being the only way to get to heaven that they tend to meet up with enmity. Such a claim stokes the ire of hell and invites the prince of this world to fiercely oppose and oppress those joined with the Lord. Relativism is a powerful brush in Satan's deceptive hand that he uses to paint all religions as efficaciously equal in the eyes of the world.

The devil will even use those closest to us to dampen and discourage our allegiance to Christ. Jesus gave His followers a heads-up in that even familial relationships possess a natural propensity for dissension and conflict as a result of both believers and nonbelievers residing under the same roof (see Luke 12:51–53).

The same can be said of how believers must exist within a postmodern, post-Christian society that has a growing agenda to "lose its religion." Eugene Peterson states, "Our times are not propitious for worship. The times never are. The world is hostile to worship. The devil hates worship ... worship must be carried out under conditions decidedly uncongenial to it."[42]

The last time that identifying with Jesus resembled anything close to being socially or culturally cutting edge, many of those who did the following ended up deserting Him or risked being deserted themselves! In other words, has identifying with a suffering Saviour *ever been* socially advantageous to the committed follower of Christ? The apostle Paul taught a long time ago that persecution would be par for the course for those who'd choose to walk a godly course in life (2 Timothy 3:12). Simply, anyone who stands for Jesus and His kingdom and claims the

[41] Steven James, introduction to *The Imitation of Christ*, by Thomas à Kempis (Orlando: Relevant Books, 2006), xi.

[42] Eugene H. Peterson, *The Message: The Bible in Contemporary Language* (Colorado Springs: Navpress, 2002), 2236.

Word of God as their compass for absolute truth risks not only ridicule but desertion in the secular realm.

The Lord explained why this is so: "If the world hates you, keep in mind that it hated me first. If you belonged to the world, it would love you as its own. As it is, you do not belong to the world, but I have chosen you out of the world. That is why the world hates you" (John 15:18–19).

In the present we are to endure *rejection* for the cause of Jesus's gospel. However, when serving the Lord in this life is all said, done, and accounted for, we can expect to gain a fully realized *redemption.* In heaven we'll marvel at the glorious presence of our awesome redeemer, worship Him at His throne, and sit around His heavenly banquet table. From that perspective all the earthly rejections we will have received through the years for simply bearing the name of Jesus will fade to nothing. It's just that we're not there yet.

REFLECTIVE QUESTIONS

1. How have you handled any rejection you've experienced on account of your faith? Describe what rejection looks like to you.
2. According to the Gospels, what sorts of rejection did Jesus experience in His ministry?
3. Why might Steven James' comment in reference to Thomas à Kempis appear challenging to the Western Christian and church?
4. How often do you consider the "costs" of living for Christ? What has being His disciple really cost you?
5. In your estimation, do the sermons you hear accentuate the "cost" element of following Christ enough?
6. Do you tend to take people's rejection of Jesus to heart? If so, what kinds of feelings do you experience?
7. How did Jesus deal with rejection? What are some things we could learn from how He dealt with people who refused to believe in Him?

CHAPTER

FOURTEEN

DOING OUR BEST SERVANT IMPRESSION

Perhaps many of us wouldn't refer to ourselves as gifted evangelists. In fact it would be safe to assume that many Christians feel very average in their ability to share their faith with the spiritually lost. It doesn't help that the twin bullies of fear and intimidation seem to show up often in the schoolyards of the Great Commission. The political correctness that towers over our society's postmodern, post-Christian landscape casts a secular shadow over the sacred. Yet Jesus's commission to His disciples is compulsory for *every* born-again believer. We have a King and kingdom to serve; we have a gospel ministry to take to our neighbours, countries, and world, a gospel that demands allegiance to a holy God and that divides sheep from goats. Yet, being an ambassador for Christ is rife with personal and relational landmines.

The task of making disciples and multiplying believers has never been easy and always runs up against worldly (including satanic) obstacles and odds. That being said, Christians can take solace in knowing that they possess the presence, power, and promises of God as they go into the world to fulfill Jesus's commission.

Faithful servants, like the one pictured in the parable of the great banquet, inspire us to head down different and sometimes difficult roads with the gospel (see Acts 8:4–29). The parable's servant did a yeoman's work in his resolve to do the will of his master by packing his banquet hall with invitees. As his master's goodwill ambassador the servant went the extra mile in order to call the haves and have-nots, the hardened and seemingly hopeless alike, to come to the event. As our present age barrels towards more intensified and pervasive forms of godlessness, whereby setting the world's stage for the emergence of the antichrist, we who bear the name, light, and truth of Christ must be all the more diligent in being Jesus to the spiritually lost.

Abraham Maslow wrote "A Theory of Human Motivation" in 1943. In his theory he identified five levels of motivation (or five needs) that humanity strives to satisfy. In order, those needs are physiological, safety, belonging and love, esteem, and self-actualization.[43] Perhaps for these very reasons, humanity tends to be drawn to philosophies, movements, and causes that hold promise for bettering its emotional and spiritual well-being.

Many new teachings and ideologies have crept into North America over the last century; consequently, it's difficult for those who are sincerely searching for a meaningful and trustworthy path in life to actually find one. Truth is, as humanity intrinsically pursues needs relating to the physiological, safety, belonging and love, esteem, and self-actualization, *truth* is often the first casualty! Those of us who know Christ and serve His kingdom require a steadfast faithfulness that will offset ideas and ideologies alienated from Scripture and spiritual truth.

No matter how interesting and even positive some spiritual teachings and philosophies may sound, all of them, one by one, have monumentally failed to rival the heart- and soul-transforming Holy-Spirit-empowered Word of God, a Word personified in God's righteous answer (Jesus Christ) for everything that keeps humanity from hoping and even flourishing in an often dark and violent world.

There were false-alarm types of Messiahs delivering fool's-gold-like optimism for a restored kingdom of Israel *before* Jesus's first coming, as there would be *after* He rose from the grave and ascended back to the place He came from. But there remains only one true and certain hope

[43] Abraham Maslow, "A Theory of Human Motivation," *Psychology Review* 50 (1943): 370–396.

for Israel's ultimate redemption and the salvation of every manner of sinner: *Jesus!* As the eternal Son and incarnated Word (logos) of God, Jesus Christ became one of us (in solidarity with our miserable plight as sinners) in order to atone for our sin and deliver us from the enslaving power of the flesh and the wiles of Satan (see Hebrews 2:14–18).

We often hear within Christian culture today the overused phrase "It's not about us" (it's about God). Yet it's biblically clear that when it came to saving sinners and rescuing them from spiritual eternal death, God made it all about *us!* We (humanity) were the ones who strayed and are in need of His grace and forgiveness! Jesus, as the Servant of God and Saviour of the world, was faithful to seek out the spiritually sick, who needed Him to be around them, even if that meant meeting with them on *their* terms and turf (see Matthew 9:12).

Selflessly and sacrificially, the Saviour came to call us back into loving communion with our Creator and then willingly died to make that possible. The Lord left His regal and rightful throne in heaven to enter a spiritually fallen and cursed world utterly unworthy of His divinity. Jesus's heaven-appointed mission is to seek out sinners and save them from an unspeakably frightful and tormented eternity separated from God (see Luke 19:10). It is only through Christ that our spiritually terminal world can begin to find not only temporal but eternal healing and hope. Simply, Jesus will always be *the* exemplar of what faithfulness looks like when serving the kingdom of God.

Some two-thousand-plus years after the Lord commissioned His disciples to be the "go" in His gospel, that same gospel blankets every continent in the world—even as it continues to seep into every uncharted cleft and crevice of civilization. It's a gospel inviting sinners from every tribe, race, and nation to come to the Saviour in humility of faith, that they may stake their claim in His heavenly kingdom and reserve their place around His banquet table.

A GREAT AND ENDURING COMMISSION

If there is a persistent undertone to Jesus's dialogue with His closest disciples it is His reiterations that following Him means owning His burden for the spiritually lost. To be *His* disciple is to participate in His redemptive plans for the world, no exceptions and no excuses.

The American Christian missionary and author Thomas Hale writes, "No one can say: '… I'm not called to be a missionary.' … There is no difference, in spiritual terms, between a missionary witnessing in his home town and a missionary witnessing in Katmandu, Nepal. We are all called to go—even if it is only to the next room, or the next block."[44]

From the opening chapter of Matthew to the final sentence in the last chapter of John, the Gospels inform us that *becoming* a Christian has little to do with outward things. *Being* a Christian has *everything* to do with living like Jesus. When we closely observe the movements and motives inherent within His activities and itinerary in the Gospels, we see how the Lord made faithfully seeking out the spiritually lost a compulsory, if not ordinary, habit.

THE EFFECT OF "MISSIONAL" LIVING

A buzzword we in the church often employ to describe the essence of how Jesus lived is *missional*. The word *missional* is derived from the Latin *missio dei*, meaning "the sending of God." Although God is the primary agent of redemptive action in the world, He nonetheless sends those His Son redeems to join Him in that work. This is essentially what being the "go" in Jesus's Great Commission is all about: the redeemed being around those who are *not* redeemed in order that they may meet *the* redeemer! Essentially, this is what it means to do our best "servant" impression!

Granted, God's people cannot "make" disciples in the sense of convicting sinners of their sin. Only the Holy Spirit can accomplish that. However, as per Jesus's instructions when He commissioned His followers, God's people *are* expected to go "into all the world"—in addition to baptizing new believers into the Body of Christ and teaching them the truths of the faith. The goal of the Great Commission, then, isn't solely the pursuing of the spiritually lost unto salvation; the goal, rather, is the moving on of new believers to becoming fully devoted and mature disciples of Jesus Christ.

When it comes to fulfilling the Great Commission, half of the task is just showing up on the mission fields of our daily lives. The Gospels do not depict the Lord as a cocooning Saviour who was closed off in His holy quarters somewhere in the temple. Jesus, rather, was entirely comfortable

[44] Thomas Hale, *On Being a Missionary* (Pasadena: William Carey Library, 1995), 6.

with getting out and being around people—even if the company He kept was among the social dregs of His culture. A good number of these people were reputed to be *outcasts*—the kind of people other people didn't want to be anywhere around!

However, as the Lord met and socialized with "obvious" sinners, the truth in Him had a way of rubbing off on them. Those most drawn to Jesus were more likely to be influenced by what He was saying and doing. Whether the spiritually lost person was deemed an outcast, outlaw, misfit, or halfwit mattered not to the Saviour, and so it shouldn't to the Christian evangelist. What matters to Jesus is that His commissioned disciples righteously impact those who, regardless of their station in life, need to be saved. Quite often this requires a little time and the formation of a trusted relationship. This cannot happen, however, if God's people are unwilling to "walk across the room" to reach those who need Christ.

Thankfully, God goes with us whenever and wherever *we* go for Him and promises to bless our efforts and faith! "And surely I am with you always," Jesus assured His disciples (Matthew 28:20). With the missional power of the Holy Spirit at their ministry's back, God's people can accomplish more than they could ever imagine possible (Ephesians 3:20).

Many of us have personally experienced how a steadfast witness for Christ can affect even those who harbour contempt towards Christianity and organized religion in general. Being a witness for Jesus means more, of course, than merely speaking for Him; a witness is also something we as Christians observably *are.* As the saying goes, we need to show lost sinners a sermon, not just tell them about one. The spiritually lost are not only listening to us; they're watching us as well! The best way to short-circuit our ministry to those without Christ is to fail to back up our evangelistic words with appropriate actions.

God's desire is for His church to go beyond merely *preaching* the gospel to *displaying* its salt-and-light peculiarities in their lives so that it may result in the spiritually lost experiencing His goodness and glory (Matthew 5:16).

In their book *Simple Church*, authors Thom Rainer and Eric Geiger comment, "The vision Jesus articulated to His disciples is that the kingdom of God will be such an influential and powerful movement in the culture that ... [people] will come and rest and receive shelter ... His desire is that the cities, the communities, and the neighborhoods where our churches are planted will benefit from our faith regardless if they believe what we believe ... or live by the values of our kingdom."[45]

STAYING THE MISSIONAL COURSE

In the course of our everyday lives, we can lose sight of the burden Jesus carries for lost sinners. For a lot of believers, looking for opportunities throughout the day to share our faith is not at the top of our to-do list. For some Christians, the Great Commission doesn't even crack the top ten in terms of what we tend to think about each morning when we get up. We have responsibilities at home and at work. We have our own cares and concerns to deal with. We have our own fears and failures to contend with. Yet the fact that Jesus calls us to not only carry the same burden He does for the spiritually lost but do something about it challenges us to identify with a Saviour who—no matter what circumstance crowded His life—stayed the missional course!

This is why I find Luke's account of the parable of the great banquet so encouraging and yet so convicting to read. It reacquaints us with the magnanimous heart of God for sinners while realigning our divided and distracted attentions and allegiances with Jesus's priorities for His church. "Strategic planning" and "key result areas" make for impressive visioning terminology and catchy acronyms in bulletins. However, adding to the roll call in heaven and turning new believers into missional-minded disciples invariably require that God's people buy into faithfully serving Jesus's kingdom by *being* the "go" in the gospel.

Problems will always plague our lives, will always be there for us to pray through and hopefully get through. We'll always be pressed for time and in need of more strength and wisdom. But the spiritually lost will always need to be ministered to as well. Unfortunately, disciples are not born; they have to be made. Disciples making other disciples isn't just the Lord's "Plan A" in accomplishing the Great Commission—*it is His plan* for His people! If we can remember that we serve a faithful God, believe in a gracious Saviour, and possess a powerful Holy-Spirit-backed gospel, we have all we need to stay our missional course. We should never doubt or fail to be surprised by what God can and will do as we go for Him!

[45] Thom S. Rainer and Eric Geiger, *Simple Church: Returning to God's Process for Making Disciples* (Nashville: B&H Publishing, 2011), 252–253.

As was the case with the servant in the parable of the great banquet, we too may find the poor, diseased, and destitute around us more spiritually open to our gospel invitation than the healthy, wealthy, and self-proclaimed wise are. Yet God is just as interested in saving the happy in life as He is the humbled and hard-done-by. He expects the sum of our lives to be about pursuing the eternal good of others around us who are separated from Him. We all have a testimony to tell and a Saviour to sell! Our lives are instruments and agencies for Christ to live His through.

Authors Francis and Lisa Chan write, "Life is about Jesus. We are not here to tell our story, but His. We are here to live His story, not ours … I have been loved, pursued, and saved by Almighty God … I will one day be swept away by Jesus into a glorious eternity. But for now I am on a mission to tell His story to others."[46]

OBSTACLES RELATED TO GOING FOR JESUS

There are times when we'd prefer that an omnipotent and sovereign God do all the work necessary to advance His kingdom—after all, it's *His* kingdom. Yet Scripture testifies that God does very little on earth without His people chipping in. The church isn't gifted to evangelize just for it to sit on its servant hands while the Almighty does the heavy lifting of saving souls. Reaching spiritually lost people for Christ can be an extremely rewarding experience—one like none other.

Sometimes it's a matter of believers possessing misplaced spiritual priorities. It's not that we don't pray for the spiritually lost or financially support ministries that endeavour to reach the unsaved; we're challenged, rather, by the "go" portion of Jesus's commission.

It doesn't make matters any easier for followers of Jesus knowing that we're living in a time of increasing moral degeneration and reconstructed Sodoms and Gomorrahs. Add to that the new barbarian presence upon the earth of organized and mobilized terrorism, and it's no wonder that the church of Jesus Christ would rather huddle together in the safety of its light than stand amid all the spiritual darkness and expose it by means of that same light.

There is a plethora of "new-world" realities associated with our postmodern, post-Christian society that form tremendous challenges to

[46] Francis and Lisa Chan, *You and Me Forever: Marriage in Light of Eternity* (San Francisco: Claire Love Publishing, 2014), 62–63.

evangelizing in the twenty-first century. The terrible persecution of God's people overseas and the escalation of legal challenges to religious liberties here in the West are soul-jarring reminders of the growing constrictions upon the church, which Jesus Himself warned would only intensify in the last days.

The melding of our national borders, cultures, and religious belief systems has led to a globalized worldview that's grown increasingly intolerant of the exclusive claims inherent within Christianity. It's long been established that the Western church feels as though it's losing its voice and influence in culture. From lawsuits to have "In God We Trust" removed from all American currency, to Supreme Court decisions that result in the removal of crosses and the Ten Commandments from public locations, to atheistic lobbyists preventing governments from speaking Christian prayers, to amendments to constitutionally based religious freedoms, to the redefining of gender identity and the definition of marriage, to the disregard for the sanctity of life and the unborn, God's people feel at times like we're up against the ropes of oppression as we do our best to endure and obey the "go" in Jesus's gospel.

PERSONAL CHALLENGES TO GOING FOR JESUS

If you're like me, you experience intervals in your faith when you feel diminutive in the midst of the largeness of our world's indifference to spiritual absolutes and religious values. Challenges and weakness always seem to surround our loyalty and service to God. Oftentimes, God permits such trials on purpose (or, shall I say, for *His* purposes!).

Remember Esther's desperate cries for justice on behalf of her fellow people of Israel before King Xerxes? Remember how God shaved off almost 90 percent of Gideon's army as Israel was about to wage war against the mighty Midianites? Remember Paul's persistent "thorn" in his "flesh" and how God refused to take whatever that thorn was away? Remember Moses's droning complaints about being too inadequate to go toe-to-toe with Pharaoh? What about the death threats and close calls Jeremiah experienced at the hands of Israel as he called them back to righteous living before the Lord?

The Bible tells us that the important thing wasn't those servants and the challenges they felt were too astronomical to overcome in serving

God. Rather, God's overriding strength and the measure of His sovereign power and will to win the day counted in the end.

Consider how the Lord called many obscure individuals to follow Him in discipleship who didn't exactly have the "right stuff" to win friends and influence people for the gospel. None of them possessed theological degrees; none of them had shelves lined with textbooks on practical ministry or resumés demonstrating any prior experience in what God was calling them to do; and neither did the early believers who made up Jesus's church! What they all had in common, however, were the unfailing promises of God, in tandem with the power of God in their midst, fuelling their ministries. The Bible wants us to be assured that the Holy Spirit equips and enables us to do what only *we* as His commissioned people are called to do; the rest we leave in God's capable hands to take care of!

You may feel (and you'd be in good company if you did) that you're not holy, worthy, gifted, or obedient enough to even begin to think about being the "go" in Jesus's gospel. When such thoughts badger our motivation to minister for Christ, keep in mind that our lives are not test drives to God. He has called many a wilting servant whom He walked with and empowered to carry out ministry tasks for His glory. When it comes to dealing with human deficiencies and our doubts concerning His choosing of us, God has been there and done that more times than we could possibly count!

Truth is, none of us are angels or demons. We're not as good as others think we are, and we're not as bad as we could be. We get some things right and other things wrong. We bring joy to the heart of God, and we grieve Him all the same. As hard as it can be for us to comprehend, God enlists and uses weak and imperfect people to accomplish His redemptive agenda in the world. He's even used individuals who refused to acknowledge Him to fulfill His righteous purposes (such as Cyrus, see Isaiah 45). So if God chooses to use those who don't even know Him to serve His redemptive plans, surely He will use those who do, including those who struggle (even mightily) in their spiritual life. We need to get over ourselves and our perceived self-inadequacies, because God has!

If you were to save someone from certain death I doubt that the person would be concerned about whether you have significant personal shortcomings. Every human being currently in a spiritually lost state could use someone like you and me (as flawed as we are) to tell them that they're absolutely adored by God. Only an unconditionally loving, unequally gracious, and unfathomably merciful God could go to such an unthinkable length as the cross and pay such an unimaginable price as the death of His Son on that cross in order to reveal the exact worth of a sinner's soul. Sadly, there are countless numbers of people all around us who still haven't heard this *Good News.*

THE GOSPEL: AN INVITATION FOR ALL TO "COME"

God's longing for His unscrupulous exiled people of Israel to return to Him—as heard through the prophet Isaiah—is a call that extends even to the spiritually lost of the twenty-first century world: "Come all you who are thirsty, come to the waters; and you who have no money, come, buy and eat! Come, buy wine and milk without money and without cost. Why spend money on what is not bread, and your labor on what does not satisfy? Listen, listen to me, and eat what is good, and you will delight in the richest of fare" (Isaiah 55:1–2).

The spiritual blessings God offers those He redeems are pictured as a banquet spread that can be partaken of "without cost"; in fact, the death of His Servant (see Isaiah 53:5–9) *paid* for the free banquet (salvation)! I challenge you to read the parable of the great banquet often and to prayerfully consider your mission field. May our days be preoccupied with thoughts of who our Master in heaven may be sending us to as His servant to invite to His heavenly banquet. Above all, may our Lord one day pronounce us as having been good and faithful at doing so!

REFLECTIVE QUESTIONS

1. What makes the Christian faith and belief system so unique among spiritual movements and other religions?
2. Define what the term *missional living* means to you.
3. Using your discretion, share some difficult experiences you've had when discussing your faith in Jesus with nonbelievers or people of a different faith.
4. List some of the challenges you feel the church faces as it attempts to preach Christ in a postmodern, post-Christian culture and world.

5. What evidence exists to suggest that your church is living out the various components of the Great Commission in Matthew 28?
6. How often do your perceived personal inadequacies and limitations affect your representing and serving the Lord?
7. What topics or themes within the parable of the great banquet affected and challenged you the most in this study?

AFTERWORD

WILL YOU ACCEPT THE BANQUET INVITATION?

Imagine with me what would happen if Jesus hadn't died for sinners. The implications are actually quite frightful. If Jesus hadn't died for our sin, we'd have no chance of escaping a hopelessly terrifying encounter with a holy God at His judgment seat (see Hebrews 9:27, 10:26–27, 31). But, praise God! Jesus did indeed die for sinners, and by our faith in Him we can begin to know the living God and avoid being separated from Him for eternity after our physical death.

Contrary to the typical bride, the church often finds herself woefully unready for that moment when she'll be united with her groom (Christ). Yet God wills to go beyond simply declaring sinners righteous and forgiven before Him; He also wills to clean up our present unkemptness due to the abiding sin nature within us. As the church we *are* the bride of Christ *now*, even as we contemplate and prepare for the consummation of our marriage to the Lord and its subsequent celebration, the marriage feast of the Lamb.

The moment is approaching when Jesus will reappear at His second coming to show that He has not forgotten His oppressed people of Israel. In fact, the Saviour could never be satisfied with leaving the world He loves captive to the enslaving wiles of Satan. Jesus was born as not only the king of the Jews but also the king of *all* earthly kings. A heavenly host of angels descended to the outskirts of Bethlehem proclaiming in unison that His kingdom had come. At His very birth our Lord was recognized as a king. In a forlorn makeshift delivery room that took over an animal stable, lowly shepherds bowed down to Him. Worship and honour were the soundtrack of the Incarnation of Christ and His accompanying kingdom.

Yet many today are still asking, "Where is this kingdom? If Jesus is king over all, where is He now?" Thankfully, God's Word possesses a great answer to such a good question!

When Jesus Christ emerges both visibly and ominously on earth's ill-prepared stage, He'll do so accompanied by heavenly angels at His sovereign disposal in order to fulfill every iota of His kingdom's agenda, a kingdom without end, and one He'll rule over forever. All other earthly kings, kingdoms, and powers will blow away like lint on a windy day (see Matthew 24:30–31; Revelation 19:11–16).

The Bible affirms many times the fragile and finite essence of humanity. We are but a moment's "mist" that will one day "vanish" (James 4:14). Humans resemble a single "breath," and all their days amount to "a fleeting shadow" (Psalm 144:4). We're a vapour that comes and goes like a "passing breeze" (Psalm 78:39). "[We] come from dust, and to dust all return" (Ecclesiastes 3:20). As a collectively sinful and broken human race that daily stands on the precipice of death and eternity, we are in desperate need of the only Saviour and Healer: the eternal one, Jesus Christ!

Dear reader, you may feel as though you're trapped and undone spiritually, like you can't be the person God wants you to be. But, praise God, Jesus *can* make you that person! When we ask Him to be our Saviour and King and to reign in our hearts and lives, He saves us and frees us from the dictating power of sin. No one who has ever come to Jesus in contrition and by faith heard Him say, "No, not you." Or, "You lose." Or, "Sorry, you're too late. Heaven's full." A big-hearted Saviour died for us, the same big-hearted God who welcomes you (indeed everyone) right now. God's invitation to us to enter His kingdom and sit at His banquet table is granted by sheer grace, a grace He does not *owe* any of us.

Yet God so loved the world that He gave His one and only begotten Son—the great liberator and all-sufficient rescue plan God initiated in eternity past—to save sinners (including Israel) from spiritual, eternal death. Jesus wanted His fellow Jewish people to come to redeeming terms with that truth and consequently exhibit a saving faith in Him. Many more of them didn't than did.

Preparations for the great future eschatological banquet will soon be finalized. It'll be a feast unmatched by even the highest earthly standards, with its central honoured figure being one (Jesus Christ) who is wholly unlike anyone else who has ever existed, whether in heaven or on earth. The heavenly table is being set; the menu is surely delectable, varied, and all-satisfying. The RSVP list is growing even as more invitations are being sent out.

It's an event our souls simply cannot afford to miss, for to miss it is to miss out on heaven entirely. Countless numbers of people will be there, from the most popular patriarch to the most prolific apostle; from the most infamous of saved sinners to the most insignificant of God's servants; from the greatest in the kingdom to the least of those who were once lost but have now been found in Christ. The question remains, however: Will *you* be there? Have you *truly* accepted the invitation the Servant (Jesus Christ) extended to you? Your answer will determine whether or not you're kingdom-bound and wedding-banquet ready.

New From
Castle Quay Books

THE
TRUE STORY
OF CANADIAN HUMAN
TRAFFICKING
BY PAUL H. BOGE
FOREWORD BY PAUL BRANDT

GENERAL EDITORS
JOHN BOWEN
& MICHAEL KNOWLES
GOOD NEWS CHURCH:
CELEBRATING THE LEGACY OF HAROLD PERCY

AM I SAFE?
Exploring Fear and Anxiety with Children
Includes a Discussion and Activity Guide and a special feature from singer/songwriter Steve Bell
BLESS YOU
WRITTEN BY IONA SNAIR AND TIM HUFF
ILLUSTRATED BY TIM HUFF

Faith,
LEADERSHIP
and Public Life

Leadership Lessons
from Moses to Jesus

Preston Manning

www.ingramcontent.com/pod-product-compliance
Lightning Source LLC
Chambersburg PA
CBHW051735090426
42738CB00010B/2261

9781988928036